THE JOYS OF RAISING

BOYS

The Good, the Bad, and the HILARIOUS

A ~~MEMOIR~~ MOMOIR by DIANE AUTEN

Foreword by JEAN STEEL of *Happy People Win*

Additional Praise For
The Joys of Raising Boys

Diane Auten is one of the cleverest, caring and lovingly sarcastic writers I know. Her fantastic tales of being a mom to two comical outspoken boys make you not only want more, but also to be personally invited to her house so you can witness the hilarity of this tight knit family yourself. This book is a laugh out loud page turner.

—**Hayley Townley**,
Author of *There Is Life After Breast Cancer*

Diane's "momoir" offers a hilarious behind the scenes look at the life of a mom raising all boys. Her daily conversations with her sons will have you in stitches and make you want to start chronicling the funny and heartfelt things your own children say.

—**Jennifer Martin**,
Co-Author of *The Unofficial Guide to Surviving Life with Boys* and creator of momvstheboys.com

The raw anecdotes of Diane's family are an absolute riot! She captures an unfiltered view of parenting in all its awkward, challenging glory, yet includes the *love* too! As a mom to one little girl so far, trust me when I say you don't need to have boys to find these stories absolutely hilarious! Though some of her stories do have me hoping for all girls. Enjoy!

—**Nicole Page,**
MomFire Blog Creator at momfire.com

Diane nailed this lighthearted and one of a kind memoir. While you will laugh at all of her funny stories and quotes, you can also feel her deep connection with her sons. *The Joys of Raising Boys* will not only make you smile, but will also simultaneously give you insight on how to communicate better with the boys in your life.

—**Michelle Sorro**,
Television Host and Author of *The Voice of Gratitude: Celebrating the Gift of Friendship*

Diane Auten's delightful book will entertain, amuse, and even painlessly educate the reader on how to improve communication within their family. She shifts effortlessly between roles of "mom" and "communication expert," as she integrates solid communication guidelines into her descriptions, explanations, and stories.

—**Michael Fahs, Ph.D.**,
Communication Professor Emeritus, Cal Poly San Luis Obispo

If you have ever wondered what it is really like raising boys, then look no further than Diane Auten's momoir, *The Joys of Raising Boys*. These stories will have you laughing and wondering how she survived. Her ability to connect so well with her boys will warm your heart and leave you in stitches!

—Beth Giusti,
Mom blogger at *Real Life Mama Drama*

This book is a must read for any boymom! It's hilarious, heartfelt, and very relatable. Although raising boys is an adventure and sometimes difficult, Diane does a wonderful job describing the fun of being a boymom. I guarantee this book will make you laugh and will help you understand the joy that comes with raising boys."

—Tiffany O'Connor,
Co-Author of *The Unofficial Guide to Surviving Life with Boys*

I absolutely adore and appreciate Diane's approach to parenting. To keep our sanity as parents, we have to utilize humor and honesty while raising our children. In *The Joys of Raising Boys,* Diane captures both of these qualities brilliantly!

—Echo Aspnes,
The Mad Mommy blogger from
TheMadMommy.com

THE JOYS OF RAISING

BOYS

The Good, the Bad, and the HILARIOUS

THE JOYS OF RAISING

BOYS

The Good, the Bad, and the HILARIOUS

DIANE AUTEN

Diane Au (signature)

AUTHOR ACADEMY elite

This book is dedicated to
the awesome pack of testosterone-laden males
at my house:
my husband, Dave, and my sons,
Bradley and Nate.
Without them and their craziness,
this book wouldn't exist.

"Having children is like

living in a frat house.

Nobody sleeps,

everything is broken,

and there's a lot of throwing up."

—Ray Romano

Contents

Foreword

I'm one of them.

Yes, I admit it: I'm one of Diane's many friends who urged her to write a book sharing her boys' hijinks. Because I, like her other friends and followers, couldn't stop laughing at all of the Auten boys exploits (when I say boys I also include her crazy husband Dave) she has shared for years on social media.

As a motivational speaker, my life passion is helping people find joy in their lives. I started my own successful business, Happy People Win, where I travel throughout the United States teaching people how to find their own happiness and reduce their stress. As a professional speaker and author, my mission has been to change people's lives for the better. And let me tell you, Diane's book will not only bring you joy, but it will also make you laugh—the perfect prescription for happiness.

Diane and I met over 10 years ago. She was (and still is) a stellar and popular communication instructor at one of our local colleges. As soon as we met, we were instant friends. Diane and I are both professional speakers, and we have had a blast presenting together over the years. A few times, we have even gotten in trouble together at speaking events when I would laugh convulsively at one of her comments. I just couldn't help it; she is funny.

When you meet someone who makes you laugh, you gravitate towards them. Because let's face it—we all need laughter in our lives. And when that friend has freaking hysterical kids, it makes the relationship that much better. I have met witty kids before, but there is something special about Bradley and Nate. They are insightful beyond their years and yes, funny as hell. I laugh often, long and hard over these two boys' antics. Because they are often unintentionally hilarious, it makes what they say even more endearing. Nothing is off limits and no one gets embarrassed.

Who knew, for example, that boys played games like "take the pain" where they had competitions to see who could withstand the pain the longest while squirting a hose down their underwear? Or that a dad played a game called "stunt baby" when they were toddlers, rolling them across the bed, yelling things like "rolling out of a speeding car!" or dangling them over the side of the bed while holding their hands, yelling "falling off the edge of a cliff!" as he let go. Well, this family did. I would watch those boys laugh and shriek with happiness, and I knew right then that they were going to grow up with a sense of humor, love of life, and a closeness with their parents. And based on this book you are about to dive into, you will see that I was right.

What you are about to read is going to bring a smile to your face. Every single pre-reader of this book said something along the lines of, "Rarely do I laugh out loud when reading a book, but this book made me do just that." Thanks Diane and the Auten boys—you make the world a happier, and funnier place.

Jean Steel
Happy People Win
Author of *I'd Like to Run Wild* and
*Need Change? Customer Service Tips to Grow
from Good to Great!*

Introduction

"Mom, Sadie is licking her *vagina!*"

"I know; it's okay. She's a dog and is cleaning herself."

Nate scrunched up his nose and asked, "Do *all* women do that?"

As you can probably tell from this exchange with my then four-year-old son Nate, we laugh a lot at my house. Although some of the things my sons say can be mortifying, we still laugh a lot. As Charles Dickens once said, "A boy's story is the best that is ever told." And just as any other boy-mom can attest, man, do I have stories.

In fact, I am fully convinced that kids are the most hysterical and entertaining beings on earth. They say and do things that make their parents want to run for the hills and hide in embarrassment, but they also give us funny stories to tell. The best part about kids is how innocent they are when they are being inappropriate. They have no idea what they are saying half the time!

Like other moms and dads navigating the waters of parenting, when my sons Bradley and Nate said or did funny things, I would post about it on social media. Many of my friends would "LOL" and leave comments about how they could relate. But it was when I started consistently posting their innocent and inappropriate quotes more often, that my friends and followers began encouraging me to write a book.

In fact, the exchange about Sadie licking her vagina made me laugh uncontrollably, and of course, I immediately had to share it on social media. I had hundreds of people laughing, commenting, and sharing this post, and it was this exact post that made me take the plunge into writing this book.

In the beginning, I was writing this book just for my family. My goal was to save all of our funny exchanges so I could share them with the boys and their families when they were older. As I worked on this project, cataloging and sharing on social media, it became increasingly clear that other people may find joy in our exchanges as well. Hence, I am sharing this with you.

A funny exchange happened recently when I walked by the bathroom and saw Bradley standing up peeing while reading a book. I couldn't believe my eyes and told him that he was going to get pee all over the floor, and he needed to pay attention to what he was doing. He just looked at me like I was crazy, and said, "Mom, I have been standing up peeing for ten years. I think I've got it."

These kinds of scenarios were the impetus for me to start keeping track of the crazy questions my boys asked, as well as the funny observations they had about the world around them. On my journey of recording our exchanges, the types of questions they asked started to evolve.

As the boys began learning more and more about their bodies (and noticing things about my body that were different), their questions and comments became funnier. Seeing a human body through the eyes of little men is quite entertaining! For example, when Bradley (four) asked me when he was going to get "hairballs on his tenders like dad." I mean, come on; that is just a hysterical way to word that question.

I should also mention, I am a full-time college professor with both a bachelor's and master's degree in communication studies, so communicating is in my DNA. For over two decades, I have enjoyed teaching others how to connect with people in their lives so they can have more satisfying relationships through effective communication. As soon as my boys started talking and interacting, I tried my best to model effective, connective conversations and to subtly teach them how to form solid relationships.

Now that my boys are older (12 and 14), communication is still part of our day. They still walk through the door after school, throw their backpacks on the floor, put away all cell phones, sit on the couch, and are ready to talk. Since they have gotten older, we also started doing this at night before they go to sleep. We always spend the last 30 minutes of the day talking—them in their beds, me in a chair, the lights off in their bedroom and us just talking. They get upset when we have a hectic day and can't do this. They say it helps them sleep. I believe this is probably true.

Many communication specialists suggest that most boys (and men) feel more com-fortable communicating side-by-side, versus face-to-face. Watch little boys play, and you see a lot of parallel play, side-by-side. Most girls play face-to-face. One strategy I always use to get my boys to converse is to find opportunities to talk in the dark, where they don't have to look at me. It can be anything from driving in the car at night (this is one of my favorites) to talking with them in the dark before bed time. I feel this is why my boys are highly effective communicators now; they practiced these skills all along. What a gift this is for their future relationships.

I have always had an open and honest relationship with my boys. My rule was and is the following: if you have a question about something, ask me and I will always tell you the truth. Boy, did they take me at my word!

For example, one day Nate asked me, "Mom, are you going to have any more babies?" "No, I can't. Your dad had a vasectomy." "What's a *vasectomy*?" "It's like a little operation where the doctor cuts the tube where the sperm comes out of a man." "Dad had his tenders cut?" "Yes." Nate, flying down the hall to the living room, "Bradley! You will never believe it! Dad has a *vagina!*"

Obviously, the exchange above required a more detailed conversation.

These ongoing open conversations built trust between my boys and me and laid a solid foundation, one that has also paid off now that they are older and still talk openly with me. It's this ongoing honesty that has led to many of the dialogues between us that you are about to read. It took me over 10 years to catalog the hilarious things they said.

Finally, all conversations you are about to read in this book were authentic exchanges between my sons and me (and sometimes my husband, Dave) when they were between the ages of two and 10. The furry babies you will read about in our stories include our dogs Sadie (yellow lab), Rowdy (red lab), and Chico (Chihuahua).

I also need to make clear that my boys are great human beings. In addition to being funny and sweet, they are kind, loving, and polite people. I feel like I need to mention this because you may get a different impression while you are reading our conversations, so I will sprinkle in some of their sweet stories as well. One example is when we went around the table at Christmas saying what we were thankful for and Nate (four) said, "I am thankful for my belly button."

When I told the boys that I was writing a book about them, Bradley (14) said, "If you make any money, I want half!" and, "Please don't post any more pictures of me on Facebook in my underwear." Nate (12) said, in his normally sweet way, "I don't care if people know about our life; we have a fun life."

So, there you go. I hope you enjoy reading my "momoir" as much as I enjoyed every moment of living it and writing it.

PART I

UNDERSTANDING BODIES

ALRIGHT, MY FRIEND, strap on your seatbelt because here we go. In the first section of this book, we must address what is at the forefront of most little boys' minds—their plumbing. For most of us who spend time around little boys, we know that they have a fascination (can we even say obsession?) with their penis. From an early age, they play with it incessantly, talk about it often, and have lots of questions about what it does.

As I looked through the categories of content for this book, it just made sense to start here, because let's face it—it's of top importance in the boy world. In fact, when doing a Google search for funny quotes about little boys discovering their private parts, multiple pages reveal a variety of links entitled something similar to "Parents Share the Most Inappropriate Things Their Kid Ever Did." For people who have young boys in their lives, it may not be surprising that with one click of a button, you learn that 99% of these inappropriate things were said or done by young boys.

There are many competing theories surrounding the idea of what parents should teach their children to call their private parts. I am not here to argue for or against any of these theories, as I feel that all parents need to make the choice of what feels right for them and their family. However, Dave and I chose to follow the advice of The American Academy of Pediatrics, which recommends, "It's important to teach children the proper names for body parts. Making up names for body parts may give the idea that there is something bad about the proper name."[1]

One of Bradley's early preschool teachers and I had a conversation about this when Bradley was just learning to talk, and she made a great point, saying that his penis should be viewed as any other body part, just like his nose, hand, or toes. There are no body parts to be ashamed of.

Additionally, there is a growing movement in schools, where educators believe that teaching what linguists call "standard" dialect for body parts is important. Specialists from the National Sexual Violence Resource Center state that "when children are taught the anatomically correct names for their body parts, it

Boys Exploring Their Bodies

Showing That We Were Fit Parents

AS YOU CAN imagine, when you have two young boys, their "tenders" as my boys sometimes liked to call their private parts, were a huge fascination and topic of discussion. When Bradley was about to turn five-years-old, he had a particular fascination with his penis. He always either had his hands down his pants or was talking about his penis.

Right after Bradley's fifth birthday, we hosted a foreign exchange student from

Indonesia. We were so excited to welcome this young man into our lives and to introduce the boys to 14-year-old Bayu and all of his cultural differences.

Before we were officially allowed to host Bayu in our home, however, the woman from the host agency had to come visit us at our house to make sure that we were "suitable." She had to make sure we were stable adults, our house was safe, and she had to meet Bradley and Nate. We not only cleaned our house to perfection, but we also made coffee and cookies, dressed in our best clothes, and gave our boys a stern talking to, "You two better be on your *best* behavior. No fighting, interrupting, or craziness. We have to show this woman that we are nice people." "Okay, Mom." I got from the boys (a little too quickly, I might add).

Once the woman knocked on the door, and the niceties exchanged, we sat down to answer her questions and make a positive first impression. Bradley was acting up a little bit, so I quickly gave him *the look* and he quieted down and sat in the corner of the living room. We went along answering her questions for about 15 minutes until I realized that it was much too quiet. I broke eye contact with her and quickly scanned the room looking for Bradley.

I spotted him in the corner of the living room, with his pants pulled down around his ankles, happily playing with his erection. I immediately turned crimson red, jumped up, and tried to cover him as the woman just laughed. "I'm so sorry," I said over and over again, mortified beyond belief, and sure that we had blown the interview and would never get to meet Bayu.

She laughed for what seemed like forever and had the perfect response: "Don't worry, I understand; I have four sons."

And just like that, we were given the green light to be a host family.

Mystery Parts

Nate (in a panic): "Mom! Something is wrong with me!"

Me: "Are you okay? What's the matter?"

Nate: "I have these two hard bubbles growing under my penis!"

On Rubbing Your Junk on the Carpet

Bradley: "Mom, why does Chico lay on the ground with his back legs out behind him and drag himself around on the carpet?"

Me: "Well, I suppose he is rubbing his penis on the ground when he crawls like that, and he likes it."

Bradley (after thinking about it a little bit): "Can I try that, too?"

On Being Multilingual

Nate: "Mom, is the word *penis* Spanish for *hot dog*?"

On Getting a Little Too Excited

Nate (at the breakfast table this morning): "Mom, I have an erection."

Me: "Well, that's lovely. That's not usually something you just announce, by the way."

Dave: "Nate, think about some ducks in the water, that's what your mom always tells me. It will make it go away."

Nate: "Why do I have it?"

Me: "Well, most of the time when adult men get erections, it is because they are excited, but with yours, it's most likely because it is morning."

Nate: "No, I am really excited; I am excited about my birthday. That's why I got it."

On Sibling Rivalry

Bradley (six) yelling down the hallway: "Mom, Nate has a small wiener!"

Nate (four) also yelling down the hallway: "No I don't! My wiener is big!"

Bradley: "No, it's not! My wiener is way bigger than yours!"

They went back and forth, back and forth, until I finally yelled without thinking:

"Both of your wieners are big, so quit fighting about it!"

#modelparenting

The Enduring Fascination with Wedgies

Me: "Bradley, what did you learn in kindergarten today?"

Bradley: "I learned how to give a wedgie."

And just a few months later...

Bradley: "Mom, can we put some underwear on the dog and give her a wedgie?"

And then there's Nate's take on wedgies...

I walked in to Nate (five) sulking with a sad face.

Me: "What's wrong, baby?"

Nate: "I gave myself a wedgie that was too hard and now my butt hurts."

On Bradley's Political Opinion

While watching TV, some commercials came on for the sheriff candidates and their appeals. Dave and I were talking about how they needed some help in the communication department, and how they needed to work on the delivery of their message.

Then Bradley chimes in with, "Their messages were fine, but they are super nervous. They just need a good wedgie."

We All Need Private Time

Me (talking to Nate who was spending a ton of time in a fort that he had built): "What the heck are you doing in there?"

Nate (four): "I am sitting in here with my hands down my pants where nobody will bother me."

Itching for Something to Do

Bradley (one rainy day): "I am so bored. I need to find something else to do besides itch my frank-and-beans."

On Wanting to be a Man

Bradley (four): "How old do I have to be before I get a nest of hair on my nuts?"

On Interesting Menu Options

The first time we took the boys to a restaurant, we were cautious, to say the least. Our boys were great kids, but they could also be very verbal, and would often blurt out embarrassing things when we were in public. They had a habit of talking about their "tenders" (or private parts) to anyone who would listen and would sometimes ask random overweight women if they were pregnant. These were things we were working on.

So, as we sat down in the restaurant and the menus were handed to us, Bradley (four) asked me to read the menu options to him. I started listing off the options saying "they have a cheeseburger, pasta, peanut butter and jelly, or chicken tenders." At the mention of chicken tenders, Bradley gasped and immediately yelled: "They serve chicken penises on the menu?" Of course, everyone looked at us and we had to explain that he referred to his penis as his tenders. That was the first and last time we went to a restaurant for a long while.

On Being Appropriate

Bradley: "Nate! Get your hands out of your pants! That isn't very ladylike!"

Bradley (whispering to me): "Mom, what does 'ladylike' mean?"

Surprise in Your Pants

Nate (10): "Mom, a bunch of the boys in school always whisper about getting boners during class."

Me: "Does that happen to you, too?"

Nate: "Yes."

Me: "What do you do? Do you try to hide it?"

Nate: "No, I don't care. I just walk around with my boner; if I tried to hide it, I would never be able to get up out of my seat."

On Quality Reasoning Skills

Me: "Bradley! Stop walking across the front seat of my car with your filthy shoes on! Then I have to sit in all of that dirt."

Bradley: "Well, Mom, your butt is dirtier than my feet, so what difference does it make?"

On Fish Production

Bradley: "Mom, what are testicles for?"

Me: "To house your sperm."

Bradley: "What are sperm?"

Me: "The little tadpole-like things that live in your testicles."

Bradley (wide-eyed and open-mouthed): "So fish will come out of my penis?"

On How to Describe a Butt

Nate: "Mom, what does 'baby got back' mean?"

Me: "If a person has *back* then they have a nice butt."

Nate: "Why would you call your butt a back?"

Me: "I don't know…it's a slang word."

Nate: "Like 'junk in the trunk'? Does that mean the same thing?"

Me: "Yes, they mean the same thing."

Nate: "A butt is not a back, though. Why do we bother to learn about body parts in school if people are just going to mix them up?"

How Emasculating

Nate (eight) talking to his friend: "Make sure that you don't feed our new dog; he can't eat or drink because daddy is taking him to get his balls cut off."

The Perfect Hiding Spot

While looking for the missing book on CD (that Nate lost) from the library,

Me: "Okay, boys, let's think like Nate. Where would Nate hide something?"

Bradley: "Mom, I'm pretty sure the CD isn't down his pants."

Breaking a Different Kind of Ice

Me: "Isn't this fun playing *Don't Break the Ice* together?"

Nate (five): "I am so excited that I am going to hit myself in the penis with my hammer!" (He proceeds to whack himself in the penis with his hammer, which promptly drops him to his knees in pain, rolling around holding his crotch).

Me: (open-mouthed and wide-eyed, looking at Bradley): "What is *wrong* with you people?"

For the Love of Friction

Bradley (five): "I like to dry myself off after a shower because I can rub my penis as much as I want to with no underwear on."

Multitasking is an Art

Sitting at breakfast, Nate (three) was eating with one hand and *enjoying himself* with his other hand down his pants.

Dave: "Nate!" You can't play with your penis while you are sitting at the counter eating!"

Bradley (five): "Just go in the bathroom and lock the door and do it, that's what I do."

On Having a Broken Penis

Nate: "Mom, I have bad news for you."

Me: "What's wrong?"

Nate: "My penis is broken. Instead of hanging down like usual, it is sticking straight out."

Bradley Practicing Puns

Me (noticing Bradley sitting with his hands down his pants): "Bradley, what's up with the party in your pants? You need to go in private."

Bradley: "Well Mom, these pants are awesome because they have a big hole in the pocket where my hand can reach through."

Me: "Well, take them off then, and we'll throw them away."

Bradley: "*No way!* These are my favorite pants! They make things *handy.*"

Ask Again in a Few Years

Bradley (five) getting out of the shower: "Mom, is my penis an important part of my body?"

Me: "Hmm... I don't know. What do you think?"

Bradley: "Not really."

Me: "Just give it a few years; your opinion may change."

Kids Talking Too Much

You learn a lot working in a kindergarten classroom. When I was leading a math group in Nate's class, a little girl told us, "We went to Disneyland and my mom and dad went on Pirates of the Caribbean alone together. My dad got so scared that his pants burst open, and when they got off the ride, his pants were open and unzipped."

Nate turned to me and said, "Has that ever happened to you and Dad?"

On Getting Excited

Bradley (in bed, yelling from the bedroom): "Mom, these covers on top of me are making me hot!"

Me: "Well, take them off then!"

Bradley: "Not that kind of hot...the *other* kind of hot."

Now You See It, Now You Don't

Bradley: "Mom! I am worried about Chico! He has this big red thing sticking out of his penis!"

Me: "I am sure he is fine. Just leave him alone."

A minute later...

Bradley: "*Mom!* The red thing sticking out of his penis disappeared! His penis is disintegrating! We need to take him to the doctor before his penis disintegrates all the way!"

Knives vs. Fire

Bradley: "Mom, what does your sore throat feel like?"

Me: "It feels like there are knives in my throat cutting me every time I swallow."

Bradley: "Ooh yeah, Mom. I understand that feeling. When I get soap in my penis in the shower, it feels like fire is coming out of my private parts."

On Getting Your Junk Clean

Me: "Bradley, before you get out of the shower, make sure you wash all of your private parts extra well."

Bradley: "Mom—I already put soap on my finger and put it up my butt two different times. I think it is clean."

On Chico's Grudges

In 2012, I was sitting in a beach chair at a local park, watching Bradley's soccer practice with all of the other parents. I was reading my book and enjoying the sunny day, when out of nowhere, a little white car full of people screeched up next to the curb, creaked open the rusty door, and said, "Bye, Chico!" as they tossed a little black Chihuahua out of the car. Without hesitation, they sped off leaving this sweet little dog behind.

Chico proceeded to run around the field, giving dog kisses to anyone who would accept them, and capturing all of our hearts. Needless to say, Chico became part of the Auten family.

The day after we got Chico, we took him to the vet to get a check-up, some much-needed flea medication, and to get neutered.

Later that week, I took the boys to the library, where we found a book about a dog who was abandoned and found a better family. Nate was so excited to read this book and said, "This story is just like Chico! He started with a family that didn't love him and who abandoned him, and now he is with a family that loves him, and who shows him so much attention." Bradley just sat there shaking his head, and said, "He might be mad at us, though, since we took away his favorite play toy when we took him to get his balls cut off."

On Exotic Food Choices

Bradley (10): "Mom, are you going to make that soup tonight with the ham's cock in it?"

Me: "What the heck are you talking about?"

Bradley: "You know, that soup with the beans and the cock meat that you make?"

Me: "It's not *cock*, it's a hock—a *ham hock*."

Bradley: "So, it's not penis soup?"

Me: "Um, no. It's just a bone with meat on it—a pig—you know, like bacon."

Bradley: "Thank goodness. I was trying to figure out how I was going to get out of eating cock soup."

On Enjoying Yourself a Tad Too Much

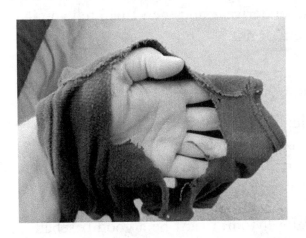

When Bradley was six, he was very attached to his underwear. He had holes the size of grapefruit in many pairs of his underwear, yet he refused to throw them away. I mean seriously—at this point, why even wear underwear?

Of course when he wasn't looking, I ditched them and bought new ones. He was so upset about it, that he refused to wear them for a while. Once he realized that the old ones were never coming back, he decided to give the new underwear a try. He reluctantly came out of his room wearing a new pair.

Me: "Do you like your new underwear?"

Bradley: "I don't know yet. I need to see if I can stick my hands down there and move things around easy like I used to be able to do with my old underwear, and then I will tell you if I like them or not."

On Getting Fresh Air

Me: "Nate, why can't you wear baseball pants to baseball practice? You are the only kid in shorts. You need to dress the part and look like a baseball player."

Nate: "Mom, I can't be a good baseball player when my tenders are sweaty and can't breathe."

···2···

How Boys Understand the Female Body

Death by Dog

WHEN THE BOYS were about seven and nine years old, we had a group of friends over for a Bar-B-Q at our house. All the kids were playing and having a great time, and the adults were enjoying some libations. At one point during the party, Bradley screamed at the top of his lungs from my bedroom, *"Chico killed a rat! Chico killed a rat!"* Of course, everybody went running to the back of the house, worried that the kids were going to get mixed up with a half-dead rat and get bitten.

We all saw Chico running around with what appeared to be a bloody rat hanging out of his mouth; the body in his mouth, and the tail hanging out the side of his mouth. All the adults were trying to catch Chico, while he just ran around and around, not willing to give up his prize. I yelled at Dave to get that damn rat away from the dog! As he was pinning the dog down, I went to grab the rat out of his mouth, and lo' and behold; it wasn't a rat at all. It was a bloody tampon he had dug out of the trash can.

#PartyOver

On the Perfect Spider's Lair

Nate: "Mom, do mommies poop out babies?"

Me: "No, they push them out of their vagina."

Then, after a long explanation of *that*,

Nate: "Do spiders move into a woman's vagina after she has a baby?"

Me: "No, Nate—why would a spider move in?"

Nate: "Well, there must be lots of room left over after the baby comes out, and it is dark in there, just like spiders like."

On Taking Things Literally

As we were unpacking from vacation and planning our week, I said to Nate, "Since you missed martial arts last week, you will have to do a makeup martial arts class on Tuesday."

Nate: "*Mom*! There is *no way* you can force me to wear makeup to martial arts!"

Boobs as a Waste of Time

Nate: "Mom, since you are done having babies, you don't need your boobs anymore, right?"

Me: "Well, yes, I guess that is true."

Nate: "When women are done with their boobs, why don't they just *decapitate* them?"

Me: "Well, women like their boobs, and in fact, many women have operations to make their boobs even bigger on purpose."

Nate: "That is one of the grossest things I have ever heard. This whole boob thing doesn't make any sense. And even weirder, Dad has boobs, too. I don't get it."

Bradley (with whom I had the sex talk) says, "Just wait until Mom has 'the talk' with you. Then it will *all* make sense."

On Hitting a Woman in the Boob

Me: "Bradley, you have to be gentle with a woman's breasts. They are sensitive."

Bradley (disgusted): "Mom, don't make me barf."

On Seeing Yourself Shirtless for the First Time

When Nate was three years old, I got him out of the bath and sat him up on the counter to brush his teeth. He looked at his naked self in the mirror for the first time, got a horrified look on his face and said, "*Mom! I have boobs!*"

We're All Just Mammals

Bradley: "Mom, why don't other girl mammals like cows and cats and stuff have to cover up their teats like human women do?"

The Boob as Food

One night, we had some friends over for dinner and one of them had a new baby. One of the second-grade boys (Bradley's age) and Bradley were talking about what the baby ate.

Bradley: "The baby doesn't eat food, it breast-feeds."

Bradley's friend (horror struck): "You can't talk about that! It is inappropriate!"

Bradley (matter-of-factly): "It's just a boob, who cares?"

Bradley's friend: "I think I am going to barf."

The Little One Takes After His Father

Bradley (walking in while I was looking at a tabloid magazine): "Look at her breasts, what's going on with them? She looks like she has big volleyballs in there!"

Nate (giggling and ogling at the picture): "I think they're cute."

The Dog and Boobs

Nate: "Mom, Chico can never be sexy; he doesn't have boobs."

On Wearing the Right Undergarments

Heading outside to play ball with the boys,

Bradley: "Mom, did you wear your running boobs today?"

Me: "I have no idea what you are talking about."

Bradley: "You know…your running boobs."

Me: "Ooh, do you mean my running bra?"

Bradley: "Yea, that's it, Mom, running boobs, so you can chase the ball."

On Oversharing

When Nate was born two months prematurely, I had to pump my breast milk and feed it to him in a bottle. Bradley would often watch me pump, fascinated. Unfortunately, he also liked to talk about it wherever we went. His favorite thing to tell people was, "Mommy's boobs are leaking."

On Discussing the Tampon Machine in the Grocery Store with Bradley

Bradley: "Mom, what's that? Is it for ladies?"

Me: "Yes, it is for ladies."

Bradley: "Do you use them?"

Me: "Yes."

Bradley: "Can I use one?"

Me: "No."

Bradley: "Would I get arrested if I use one?"

Me: "No."

Bradley: "Then *why* can't I use one?"

Me: "Because they are only for ladies."

Bradley (raising his voice with clenched teeth): "*Why?*"

Me: "Because ladies put them in their vagina, *okay?*"

Bradley (scrunching up his nose): "Well, that's just weird."

Nate's Take on the Tampon Machine, One Year Later

Nate: "Mommy, what is that for?"

Me (here we go again…): "It is for ladies."

Nate: "What do they do with them?"

Me: "Well, they put them in their vagina when they have their period."

Nate: (as he sat and stared at the stickers on the machine—one of which was the price): "Mom, why would ladies put 25 cents in their vagina?"

The Dog's Education on Boobs

Lying in bed with the boys one morning, Chico suddenly jumped up on me from out of nowhere and landed smack in the middle of my chest.

Me: "*Chico*! Ouch! That hurt! Get off my boob!"

Bradley: "Don't worry Mom. He's not touching your boob on purpose. He doesn't even know about sex yet."

On Studying Growth and Development in Fifth Grade

Bradley, Bradley's friend, and Nate were hanging out in the kitchen before school.

Bradley: "Dude! We have to miss rocket class today."

Friend: "Why?"

Bradley (groaning): "We have to go to Growth and Development class."

All three of them: "*Noooooo!*"

Me: "Listen, you two, Growth and Development is important. Make sure to ask questions if you have them. Pay particular attention to the hygiene part, because you boys are stinky."

Bradley: "This year isn't the bad year. *Next* year is the really bad year."

Me: "Why?"

Bradley: "Because we have to learn about the *other gender* in sixth grade. *Yuck!*"

Me: "You guys need to understand girls and their parts, too. It's going to be okay."

Bradley: "I already know everything I need to know about girls and their parts from when I accidentally walked into the bathroom when you were getting out of the shower after Zumba. I don't need to know anymore."

Me: "Ooh, there is a whole lot more to learn. You need to learn about how their parts work, being pregnant, all of that stuff."

Bradley's Friend: "I am going to call in sick for the whole Growth and Development week in sixth grade, so I don't have to talk about all that girl stuff."

Bradley: "Yes, I am going to barf when we have to talk about that."

Me: "Okay, boys, off to school. And remember, don't be embarrassed to ask questions today if you have them because you two are confident, outspoken young men. If you have questions, you know a lot of other kids have questions too, so ask for them."

Bradley: "I'm not embarrassed to ask questions. In fact, I am going to charge people 50 cents for me to ask a question for them. I could make a killing."

On Staying Clean

When Bradley was four-years-old, he would see our dog cleaning herself, and run up to me and say, "Look, Mom! Sadie is giving her vagina a bath!"

On Getting a Quick Education

When Bradley was in fifth grade, his class went on a field trip to the local university to learn about college. As the 100+ fifth graders walked through the quad, their teachers had a mini panic attack: Nobody had warned them that it was Sexual Assault Prevention Week on campus. Not only were there packs of college students walking around with "I love sex" t-shirts on, but someone dressed up in a full-sized vagina costume as well. The teachers tried to divert the kids' attention, but the t-shirts and dancing vagina is the only thing the students remember from the field trip. Do you blame them?

On Smelling Nice

Me (walking into the bathroom to find Nate with his head buried in the cup of my bra):

"Nate, what in the world are you doing?"

Nate: "Smelling this bra."

Me: "Why would you do that?"

Nate: "It smells delicious, like a lady."

On Padded Bras

Nate: "Mom, what are those 'boob plates'?"

Me: "I'm sorry; I'm confused about what you are asking."

Nate: "Those little pad things that were in your workout bra that you threw away."

Me: "Ooh, well some women want their boobs to look bigger than they are, so they wear pads in their bra to make their boobs look bigger."

Nate: "That is the creepiest thing I have ever heard. Boobs are gross already, why would they want them *bigger*?"

Male or Female?

Nate: "Mom, are you going to have any more babies?"

Me: "No, I can't. Your dad had a vasectomy."

Nate: "What's a *vasectomy*?"

Me: "It's like a little operation where the doctor cuts the tube where the sperm comes out of a man."

Nate: "Dad had his tenders cut?"

Me: "Yes."

Nate (flying down the hall to the living room): "Bradley! You will never believe it! Dad has a vagina!"

How Rumors Start

Bradley: "Mom, what's that one thing you were telling me about when your butt bleeds?"

Me: "What in the heck are you talking about?"

Bradley: "When your butt bleeds, you know, once a month."

Me: "Bradley, my butt doesn't bleed. It's called a *period* and comes out of the female parts, the vagina, not the butt."

Bradley: "Wait a minute. How many holes *are* there?"

Nipples are Such a Curiosity

Nate: "Mom, why do boys have nipples if they can't feed babies?"

On Copping a Feel

Nate (four) got into bed with me one morning and suddenly, I feel his hand go up my shirt and grab my boob.

Me: "*Nate!* You can't just stick your hand up a woman's shirt and grab her boob."

Nate: "I'll never get to grab a woman's boob?"

Me: "Well, yes, son, someday when you're married you can grab your wife's boob."

Nate (after a long pause): "Well, how long do I have to wait before I can get married?"

An Embarrassing Homonym

One of my friends came over for a visit with her eighth grade daughter. Bradley (sixth grade) wanted to talk with her about middle school and moving from class to class, and started the conversation asking her, "Do you have periods?" The girl got a look of horror on her face, and Bradley realized what she was thinking.

#awkward

On Relaxing at Bedtime

Nate (as I was putting him to bed): "Mom, how come you aren't wearing a bra?"

Me: "Because it is night time and I am going to bed."

Nate: "Women don't wear bras to bed?"

Me: "No, bras are about the most uncomfortable thing you can put on your body. Right when I walk through the door after work, I want to take my bra off."

Nate: "That's creepy. You should wear a bra all of the time. Moms on TV wear bras to bed. Maybe you should, too."

On Noticing Inappropriate Things at the Zoo

Bradley: "Mom! Dad took us to the zoo today, and we saw two inappropriate things!"

Me: "Well, that's just great. What did you see?"

Bradley: "First of all, there was a big statue of a tiger, and you could see its testicles!"

Me: "Well, that's not so bad. What is the second one?"

Bradley: "We were playing under a little bridge, and there was graffiti all underneath the bridge. Do you know what the graffiti said? It said, 'I like to get my nipples pinched!' What does *that* mean and why would anyone say it?"

On Drinking Breast Milk

Snuggling in bed with the boys one morning, they kept elbowing me in the boob.

Me: "Boys, you need to be a friend to the boob. It hurts when you keep jabbing me."

Bradley: "What if we don't want to be a friend to the boob?"

Me: "That boob gave you life, so you better be nice."

Nate: "What do you mean?"

Bradley: "Mom fed us from her boob, Nate. Duh."

Nate: "I drank *boob juice*? How did that happen?"

On Earning the Best Score Possible

Bradley: "Mom, can you explain the 'boob scale' to us?"

Me: "What boob scale?"

Bradley: "You know, when a lady's boobs are ranked with a number and then they earn an A, B, C, etc. Which ranking is the best?"

Me: "That's not a ranking. That is her bra size."

Bradley: "So, the lady on the show *My Strange Addiction*, who was addicted to plastic surgery and wanted to get her boobs ranked a QQQ, just wanted to make her boobs huge?"

Me: "Yes."

Bradley: "Eww! All I'm sayin' is thank God we are boys."

Don't Ogle

I was sitting on the couch with Nate, and it was very cold. I stuck my head inside my shirt to try to warm up, and Nate said, "Mom! Don't stare at your boobs. Dad said it is inappropriate to look at boobs for too long."

Small vs. Big Boobs

Nate: "Mom, how come there are girls in my 6th grade class with bigger boobs than you? They are 12 and you are 46. How is that possible?"

••• 3 •••

Teaching Boys What Our Bodies Can Do

On Lending a Helping Hand

Me: "Bradley, could you *please* not walk around naked? Nobody wants to look at all that business."

Bradley: "What difference does it make? You had to help me take a shower last year when I broke my leg, so you've already seen it all."

Me: "Well, that was an emergency situation. I am sure if I was hurt and needed help taking a shower that you would help me, too."

Bradley: "I wouldn't have to. Dad is so desperate to see you naked that he would hog all of the helping."

On Knowing When the Baby is Ready to Come Out

Nate: "Mom, when we were in your tummy, did we kick you?"

Me: "Of course you did! You kicked all of the time!"

Nate: "So did we kick our foot out of your vagina to show you when we were ready to come out? Is that how you knew we were ready?"

Just Talk Real Fast

Bradley: "Mom, guess what I learned from one of my friends at school?"

Me: "What?"

Bradley: "If you say, 'XXXXXXXXXXXXXX XXXXXXXXX' over and over again, you will actually start saying *sex*."

Out of the Birth Canal

Nate: "Mom, Bradley lied to me, and I need to make sure what he said isn't true."

Me: "Okay, what did he say?"

Nate: "He said when I was born, that I came out of your *vagina*! Is that true?"

Me: "Actually Nate, that is true. Babies are born out of their mom's vagina."

Nate (furrowing his brow): "Mom, how is that even *possible*? How can a baby fit out of a woman's vagina?"

Me: "Well, Nate, a woman's body is made to adjust so that she is able to birth a baby out of her vagina."

Nate (even more disgusted): "Is there any way that I can go back and start over and be born without coming out of your vagina? That is just gross."

Me: "Sorry, bud. It is what it is."

Nate (shook his head and walked away): "That is just so wrong."

Why Daddy Won't Leave

Me, walking into the house after the gym and finding the boys sitting on the couch:

"Where is your father?"

Them: "We don't know; he just left."

Me: "He finally got smart and escaped while he could."

Bradley: "No, he would never leave."

Me: "You're right. He would never leave. He loves you too much."

Bradley: "That's not why he wouldn't leave. He would never leave because if he leaves, he would never get to have sex again since he is old and bald."

(As you can imagine, when I told Dave about this exchange, he was none too thrilled.)

On Stinky Pits

Bradley (four): "Armpits smell like smoke and poop mixed in with everything gross."

Giving Birth to a Four-Legged Friend

Nate: "Mom, was Sadie made in your tummy like us?"

Me: "No, Sadie is a dog. She came from a dog mommy."

Nate: "People mommies can't make dog babies?"

Me: "No, Nate. That's not how things work."

Nate (thinking it over): "Well, when I get older, my wife might push out a dog baby, but not a Labrador like Sadie, though. She is too big."

On Learning New Words

The boys and I were running errands, and at one point, I parked right in front of a small store and left the boys in the car (they were 9 and 11). As I was standing in line, they set off the car alarm which caused a huge scene.

I came back to the car frustrated, and said, "What in the world is *wrong* with you people?"

Nate: "Don't have an orgasm, Mom. It's not that big of a deal."

Me: "Umm...excuse me?"

Bradley: "Yeah, don't have an orgasm over it."

Me: "Do you two even know what you are saying?"

Them (looking quizzically at each other): "No, not really."

Me: "Listen, new rule, you aren't allowed to use words when you don't know what they mean."

Bradley: "Well, what does it mean then? Is it like having a seizure?"

Me: "Yeah, something like that."

The Words You Learn in School

Bradley: "Mom, what does it mean to 'hump on something'? My friend from school says that her dog humps on her leg every day."

On Me Being Naked in Front of Strangers

Nate: "Mom, were you naked when I was born?"

Me: "Yes. Well, I had a gown on the top part, but I didn't have clothes on from the waist down."

Nate: "You didn't have pants on in front of all of those people?"

Me: "Nate, how could I give birth to you if I was wearing jeans? How would you get out? A woman has to be naked from the waist down for it to work."

Nate: "Couldn't you just pull your pants down real quick when it was time for me to come out? Didn't I just shoot out of your body like a cannon firing?"

Me (trying to speak through fits of laughter): "No, you didn't shoot out like a cannon firing. It actually takes a lot of time to deliver a baby."

Nate: "Thank goodness I never have to birth out a baby and be naked in front of all of those people. It would be way too embarrassing."

Nude Childbirth Continued...

Nate: "Was I naked when I came out of your vagina?"

Me: "Yes, you were naked."

Nate: "Were there other people in the room?"

Me: "Yes, in fact, because you were six weeks premature, there were lots of other people in the room. A ton of people were crammed in that room."

Nate: "So all of those people saw me *naked*?"

Bradley: "Yes, and they all laughed and pointed when you came out."

#BrotherlyLove

On Going on a Hunger Strike

Nate (four years old): "Mommy, how can a woman eat when a baby is filling up her tummy?"

Where Was I Conceived?

Nate: "Mom, where did you and Dad have sex when you made me?"

Bradley: "At McDonald's"

Me: "Why would you say that?"

Bradley: "Because they have such nice, big bathrooms."

On the Dog Being Playful at the Dog Park

Bradley: "Mom! Look at Chico! He is so cute—he is trying to get a piggyback ride from that other dog!"

On Being Prepared When the Situation Arises

This is what happens when your kid watches too many sports on TV and sees all of the inappropriate erectile dysfunction commercials:

Nate (10), getting in the car: "Mom, what's in this pink bag on the seat?"

Me: "Just girl stuff."

Nate: "Like what?"

Me: "Like tampons and stuff like that."

Nate: "Do you have any Viagra in there?"

Me: "Um. No. Why would I have Viagra in there?"

Nate: "In case you and Dad want to have sex in the car."

Me: "Good Lord, Nate. We are not going to have sex in the car."

Nate: "Well, tell Dad that Viagra now comes in single packs just in case."

#ThanksTVAdvertising

On Early Exposure

Me (to Dave): "Do you want to have a lunch date today while the kids are in school? We can make lunch and watch *Bachelor in Paradise*.

Dave: "Yeah, I'm in. I like that soft porn."

Nate: "What is soft porn?"

#great

Immaculate Conception

I knew after Bradley and I had the sex talk there would be some follow-up questions.

Bradley: "Mom, if I want to have children someday do my wife and I *have* to have sex? I mean, can we make a baby and not do *that*?"

Me: "Don't even worry about it, Bradley. A.) Someday you will want to do that, and B.) You will probably be begging your wife for it like most husbands."

On Being a Voyeur

Nate (watching me get dressed this morning): "Mom, why do you wear a bikini under your clothes?"

Me: "Nate, it's not a bikini, it's underwear. And you don't need to sit there and stare at me while I am naked getting dressed either."

Bradley: "Yeah, Nate. That's Dad's job."

Chico is Desperate for a Lady Friend

After Chico dug a tampon out of the trash can, for the umpteenth time,

Nate: "Poor Chico. He just wants a girlfriend so badly."

On Getting the Right Legos

When the movie *The Prince of Persia* came out, Nate was obsessed with it but called it *The Prince of Virgin* instead. Not long after, a corresponding Lego set was also released. Nate (four) saw the Lego set at the store and told his teacher (in front of his whole preschool class):

Nate: "I want the *Prince of Virgin* Legos for my birthday."

Then other kids chimed in with "I want *Prince of Virgin* Legos, too."

His teacher is going to kill me.

Who Needs a Man?

Bradley (before he fully understood how sperm works): "Mom, if sex means that a man puts his penis in a woman's vagina, then why doesn't a woman just put something else in there and be done with it? Then she wouldn't have to get naked in front of another person."

On Making Milk

Nate: "Could you make milk with your boobs right now if you wanted to?"

Me: "No. I would have to be pregnant or have a baby in order to make milk. My body would know I was pregnant and that I had a baby, and then it would make milk. Without my body knowing that, it doesn't make milk."

Bradley: "Well, every time you try to make us feel guilty about how you had to give birth to us, you say it was like pushing out a watermelon. Why don't you just stick a watermelon up there and then your body would think you are pregnant. Then you could make milk again."

On Understanding Fetishes

A few weeks after I had the sex talk with Nate...

Bradley: "Nate and I were riding our bikes today, and we saw a bumper sticker on a car that said: 'If you are going to ride my ass, at least pull my hair.' What does that mean?"

Me: "Well, that is totally inappropriate."

Bradley: "But what does that mean?"

Nate (yelling): "It's about sex, isn't it? Why does everything have to be about sex? The dogs have sex, the teenagers on our block have sex, why is everything about sex?"

Me: "I know, Nate. I am sorry, but yes, it is about sex."

Bradley: "But, what does that bumper sticker mean?"

Me: "Well, when people have sex, they are up close to each other, so when it says, 'ride my ass,' it is referring to being close enough to have sex."

Bradley: "But what about the hair pulling thing?"

Me: "Oh, for crying out loud. Some people like to have their hair pulled when they have sex, okay?"

Both boys with their mouths agape and horrified,

Bradley: "That makes *no* sense at all. They *want* someone to pull their hair? That is so *weird*!"

Nate: "Then why do we get in trouble for pulling people's hair at school, if some people like it?"

... 4 ...

Everybody Does It: Bodily Functions

The Power of Modeling

WHEN BRADLEY WAS potty training, we had a hard time getting him to poop on the potty. Peeing on the potty was no problem, but pooping was *always* an epic battle. We read an article that said the way to motivate kids to poop on the potty was to celebrate every time they did it.

This article even went as far as saying that we should "have a bathroom party" when he pooped successfully. So, as dutiful parents, we cheered Bradley on, jumping up and down, shouting when he would poop, "Good job, Bradley! You pooped! *Woohoo!*" every time he would do it. It seemed to be working. That is until our strategy backfired.

Dave was out of town one weekend, and Mervyns was having a Super Sale. Anyone who remembers Mervyns remembers their Super Sales. They were a big deal. So, one Saturday in a moment of brilliance, I decided to take the boys shopping. With a one- and three-year-old in tow, we went out to Mervyns.

The place was packed to the gills, and I had to go to the bathroom. Without any other choice, I dragged both boys into the bathroom with me. After doing my business, so to speak, I opened the door to leave, and Bradley bursts out of the bathroom door, running up and down the center aisle, shrieking and cheering, "*Mommy made a pooper! It was the biggest pooper I ever saw! Good job, Mommy!*" He was celebrating for me the way we celebrated for him. My face was as purple as a beet, and all of the people in the crammed aisles in Mervyns got a good laugh.

On Eating Excessive Fiber

While lying in bed reading with the boys, a foul stench began permeating the air.

Nate: "Mom, I have bad news for you...I ate the musical fruit earlier."

On Pooping Freely

Bradley: "Mom, I wish I was a dog so I could just stop and poop wherever and whenever I wanted, and nobody would look at me like I was weird."

On Trying to Imitate the Magic Tricks in the Harry Potter Books

Bradley: "Mom, I have a booger on the end of my finger. I am going to show you how I can make it disappear!"

Bradley: (as he proceeds to flick his booger on the floor, then shows me his "clean" finger): "*Tada!*"

On Getting the Cha-Cha-Cha

Nate (four): "Mom, I think I ate something weird that made my stomach upset because when I sit on the toilet, it is like a cannon exploding."

On Living with the California Drought

While driving in the car,

Nate: "Mom! You are in trouble!"

Me: "Why?"

Nate: "You peed on the mountains!"

Me: "What are you talking about? I did not."

Nate: "Yes you did! You peed on the mountains!"

Me: "Nate, you are crazy. I didn't pee on the mountains."

Nate: "Mom, see all of those dead spots on the mountain? They are just like in our backyard where the dog pees. Those are spots from something bigger, and you are bigger than Sadie, so you must have peed on the mountains."

On Being Constipated

Bradley: "*Mom*! I am pooping, and it hurts like I am having a baby!"

The Teachers Don't Wear Headphones

Watching the Super Bowl with friends and family,

Bradley: "I'm so excited that I can't stop farting!"

Me: "Bradley, you're gross. What do you do at school when you have to fart? Please tell me you hold it in."

Bradley: "Yep, I hold it in all day, then let them all explode out when we are in the computer lab, and everyone is wearing headphones so they can't hear."

Me: "You realize the teachers and aides in there don't wear headphones and they can hear everything, right?"

Bradley (cringing): "Oops."

On Incontinence

Me: "I jumped around too much in dance class tonight, and now my ankle hurts."

Bradley: "You jump?"

Me: "Yes, I jump around when we dance."

Bradley: "Did you pee your pants?"

Me: "Why would I pee my pants?"

Bradley: "Because I heard that after ladies have babies, when they jump, they pee their pants."

Me: "Who told you that?"

Bradley: "I saw it on TV at Aunt Jeanine's house. So, did you pee your pants?"

Me: "No, Bradley, I did not pee my pants, but I did hurt my ankle."

Bradley: "Will you tell me if you ever pee during your class when you jump around? My friends will think it is hilarious."

Brotherly Love

Me: "Bradley, when did you start sitting on the toilet to pee?"

Bradley: "Mom, I do it for a specific reason that I can't say."

Me: "What? What are you talking about?"

Bradley (after some coaxing to tell me): "I only sit on the toilet to pee when Nate has to go pee because I like to make him wait so then he pees his pants."

On Eating in Bed

Bradley: "Who was eating jam in my bed? They got jam on my pillow! Ooh, wait...it's just boogers."

Boys vs. Girls

Bradley (six) got into a disagreement with one of his (female) friends about who was better, boys or girls. Bradley's biggest argument was, "Well, boys are better to the environment because they only use toilet paper when they poop. Girls use toilet paper every time they go to the bathroom, so girls waste a lot more paper, which kills more trees, so boys are better."

The Benefits of Being Congested

Nate: "Mom, I sort of like having a cold."

Me: "Why is that, Nate?"

Nate: "With a cold and all of my snot, I can snort *way* louder."

On Bringing Home a Surprise in His Backpack

When Nate was five-years-old, I went to help him get into the bathtub to take a bath before bed. As he peeled off each layer of clothing, I noticed that he didn't have on any underwear. I knew for sure that he had underwear on when he left for school, and as a mom, I immediately panicked thinking something terrible had happened to him.

I quickly asked, "Nate, where is your underwear? I know you had underwear on earlier; if something happened to you, please tell me." Nate tilted his head to the side and looked at me like I was crazy. "Mom, nothing happened to me. I just didn't want to stop playing at recess to go to the bathroom, so I pooped in my pants."

After letting that nugget of information sink in, I probed more, "Okay, so did you throw your underwear away once you went to the bathroom at school?" Again, he looked at me like I was losing my mind and said, "No, Mom. I just took them off and put them in my backpack."

As you can imagine, horrible visions of a poop-filled backpack, poop-covered binders, and a poop-smeared lunchbox filled my head. I sat in the bathroom for a few minutes with him, trying to muster up the courage to check the level of damage I was dealing with.

Once I pulled it together, I slowly walked down the hallway to the kitchen where the backpack hung from the back of a chair. I grasped the zipper and slowly began to open it up. That's when I saw Nate's underwear, carefully rolled up into a precise, sausage-like package, preserving the perfectly formed four-inch turd in his drawers.

Just Wipe Your Butt

The boys each had a list of school supplies that they were supposed to bring to school for the new school year. On each list was a pack of baby wipes.

Bradley: "Mom, why are you sending baby wipes in my bag of supplies?"

Me: "Because I emailed your teacher and told her that you have a problem wiping your butt all the way clean after you poop. I told her to keep these on hand for you in case you get poop in your pants, and you stink."

Bradley: "*Noooooooooo!*"

Golden Showers

As I made the mistake of putting the boys (six and eight) in the shower together, they started teasing each other about their penises.

Me: "That is completely inappropriate—stop that!"

Two seconds later…

Nate: "*Bradley is peeing on me!*"

Me: "What is *wrong* with you?"

Bradley: "Well, you said not to talk about penises, not that I couldn't pee on him!"

A few weeks later, once again in the shower together,

Bradley: "Here, pee in this cup and I will pour it over your head."

Holy Flatulence

We live close to some agricultural fields and one morning farmers were fertilizing the fields. The boys were playing outside with some friends, when they all came bursting through the door plugging their noses, yelling, "It stinks out there!" Then Nate came running in last yelling, "*God farted*!"

Flu-Like Symptoms

Nate: "Mom, I think I ate something weird because I have barf coming out of my butt."

On the Perfect Boy App

While sitting in the car at Bradley's baseball practice, Nate (seven) and I decided to download the Fart Button app on my phone and proceeded to roll down the windows in the car. Every time someone walked past the car, we would press the button (on full volume), making a variety of loud, disgusting fart sounds. The people, mostly kids walking by hearing this, would look at us in horror and keep walking.

Nate and I kept looking forward as if nothing happened, and then cry-laughing after they were gone. This went on for a good 30 minutes. I swear, I have never laughed so hard in my entire life; it was like a bad episode of the TV show *Hidden Camera*.

Reflections from Mom

Having all of these conversations with my boys kept me on my toes when they were young; however, I know this level of open dialogue is not everybody's cup of tea. For us, though, it has brought us closer together.

When they were in this inquisitive stage, they made me laugh every single day with their observations and antics, and I hope they made you chuckle, too. Sometimes people would look at us sideways when my boys asked questions about their parts, my parts, or even sex. And they definitely looked at us funny when we answered them honestly.

But I always believed (and still do) that if my boys could come to me with these kinds of questions when they were young, then they could come to me about anything as they got older. When things get tougher for them as teenagers and young adults, I want them to feel that same openness and connection with me. And now that they are 12 and 14, so far, that is the case. Let's cross our fingers that it doesn't change.

PART II

RELATIONSHIPS

TEACHING BOYS HOW to love is one of the most important jobs that we have in this world. So many boys grow up unable to express themselves, whether it comes from societal influences, peer pressure, or parental shaming, it is a norm that as a society, we must turn around.

Without getting too heavy here, I am sure that most of us can agree that face-to-face communication skills are declining in our society today. A lot of us have become too dependent on technology, and many of us have lost some of the humanity of connecting with others on a deeper level—looking into someone's eyes when they talk to us, having empathy in difficult situations, and truly listening when someone is talking. This lack of connection is also rubbing off on our boys.

I don't necessarily want to go into all of the theory behind why it is harder for (most, not all) boys and men to communicate, but research shows us that it is true. The roots of empathy start early, and when it comes to nurturing empathy skills, girls have the upper hand. If you think about it, most girls grow up playing games that involve communication (think dolls, house, mommy/baby, etc.). Little girls get to practice relationship from the time they can stand on two feet.[3]

Boys, on the other hand, aren't practicing these relationship skills. They are practicing competition. Think of the games that little boys play. Most of them are "us against them" kinds of games: cops and robbers, Star Wars, any version of "bad guy against good guy," and of course, sports. While boys are growing up practicing skills around competition, the girls are leaving them in the dust when it comes to relational skills.

As a result, at an early age, I wanted to reverse some of this with my boys. Don't get me wrong—the vast majority of their childhood was spent playing competitive games. My favorite memory was when I used to walk a pack of neighborhood boys to school every morning when Bradley was in kindergarten. Every single morning they would argue about who was going to be "first leader," "second leader," and so on down the line.

I embraced this boy-way of relating wholeheartedly; however, I also wanted to nurture their relational skills. When my boys were little and wanted to watch TV or play video games, I would always say, "First, we need to have relationship time." They would moan and groan about it, but it became part of our daily routine.

"Relationship time" was when we sat with no technology and talked about whatever they wanted to talk about, but we had wonderful connective conversations. And they learned to have a balanced conversation; they learned to ask Dave and me questions about our day, and not just talk about themselves. That is an amazing skill, too.

Award-winning author and speaker Daniel Goleman, often talks about what makes a person have a successful life. He makes the argument that how knowledgeable we are, or our IQ, has very little to do with our successes in life.[4]

Remember, I am an educator, so this is a hard pill for me to swallow; however, I am a professor who teaches a variety of classes on communication, one of which focuses entirely on how to have successful relationships. Because of my background as a teacher, a parent, and someone who is exposed to college students every day, I have to agree with Goleman.

Don't get me wrong; IQ is important, but as Goleman points out, think of how irrelevant it is to life success. Our IQ has nothing to do with how successful our relationships are. IQ has nothing to do with how happy we are in our marriages, and how connective our relationships are with our kids. It takes something more than that. It takes an emotional connection to have successful relationships—with our spouses, friends, and importantly, our children.

Now before you dive into all the funny and somewhat shocking quotes in this next section, I have to tell you that my boys are very empathetic. This is something that Dave and I have worked very hard to cultivate in our boys.

For example, this past Halloween, Bradley (14) went trick-or-treating with his pack of friends, and one of his friends brought her little brother (who was in third grade) along. Not long after leaving the house to go trick-or-treating, the friend's little brother got an intense, bloody nose and had to go home.

At the end of the night, after all the kids had gone home, I went to raid some of Bradley's candy for myself (they had been out for hours, so I thought I would have a ton of candy to choose from). I looked in his bag, and noticed amongst a few empty wrappers, about 10 little candy bars nestled in the bag.

At first, I got upset thinking he had eaten all that candy, then I got mad because there was none for me! I asked Bradley what happened to all his candy, and he said he gave it to his friend to give to her little brother; he felt bad that her brother didn't get to go trick-or-treating, so Bradley wanted him to have some candy.

My friend...that is a shining example of empathy right there. Honestly, that was one of my most proud mom-moments with him. Bradley has had many empathetic moments now that he is a teenager, and he always amazes me with how communicative and emotionally healthy he is. He is not perfect—he can be a real a-hole teenager sometimes. But the big picture is that he is a great young man, and I believe that much of it stems from the open communication we had when he was younger.

Another example was when Nate was given a special award in his sixth grade class. The students voted by secret ballot on who they thought was the most kind, generous, open-hearted student in the class. According to Nate's teacher, he won by a landslide. And when his teacher presented him with the award, his fellow students gave him a standing ovation. Nate was mildly humiliated over how much I cried when they gave him the standing ovation, but I didn't care; that boy is just so sweet and loving, and it makes me feel so much joy that his peers see that as well.

Washington Irving once said, "There is an enduring tenderness in the love of a mother to a son that transcends all other affections of the heart." For most boys, his mother is his first true love. She is the person who he goes to most often for comfort, love, compassion, reassurance, and empathy. Mothers are often the emotional role models for young boys, and the mother-son relationship is significant.

My boys and I have a close bond, but let me say—sometimes my boys are *too* honest with me if that is possible. Bradley and Nate were raised in a very open and communicative home, which led them to share their opinions freely on things like when I gained or lost weight, what my hair looked like after going to the beauty salon, how old I looked, and even how weird I dressed.

This also prompted a whole discussion on how to soften a message. For example, recently, Nate asked me what a white lie was. I explained that a white lie was when someone lied to spare someone else's feelings, like when someone falls and is embarrassed, and you tell them that nobody noticed (when they did). Or, you tell someone their hair looks nice after they get it done, even if you don't care for it.

But, the exchanges you are about to read happened when the boys were younger and had no filter. Luckily, I have pretty high self-esteem, and I just laughed off the vast majority of these comments. As Bradley and Nate got older, they softened their comments to me. So please keep in mind that my boys do love me as you are reading the next chapter, even though some of the things they said to me when they were younger might make you think otherwise. Ha!

••• 5 •••

Teaching Boys About Love

On Cultivating Quality Relationships

Bradley (four): "Mom, can I play games on your phone, please?"

Me: "Instead of playing games on screens, you need to work on your relationships."

Bradley: "What's a relationship?"

Me: "A relationship is when you show you care, spend time with someone, show respect, and pay attention to them."

Bradley (as serious as could be): "Well, I like to work on my relationship with my video games."

On Being the Boss in Marriage

Bradley: "Mom, I am going to marry you when I get older so I can be the boss of you."

On Marrying the Dog

Bradley, speaking to Nate (who loves mermaids): "You can't marry a mermaid when you get older because you are going to marry Sadie."

Nate: "I could never marry Sadie."

Me: "Why, because she is a dog?"

Nate: "No, Mom. I can't marry Sadie because she can't dance."

On Mean Girlfriends

Bradley: "Mom, does 'ex-girlfriend' stand for extra girlfriend?"

Me: "No, Bradley—why would you need an extra girlfriend?"

Bradley: "In case your first girlfriend is mean. You would need an extra one as backup."

On Making Out with the Dog

Bradley: "Chico's tongue tastes like bacon."

On Being a Secret-Keeper

Bradley (six) whispering: "I am about to tell you something, but you have to promise not to tell Dad."

Me: "Okay, what is it?"

Bradley: "I am going to marry you someday so we can sleep in the same bed instead of you and Daddy."

On the Rules of Marriage

Nate (four): "Mom, how come I have to sleep by myself every night when you and daddy always get to sleep together?"

Me: "We are married. When you are married to someone, you share everything, even your bed."

Nate: "I am going to marry Bradley then. He always has good toys, and then he will be forced to share them with me."

On a Boy's First Kiss

Me: "Bradley, please go get in the shower."

Bradley: "Hold on. I need to make out with Chico first." (And the tongue kissing commences)

Me: "Bradley! Stop sticking your tongue in Chico's mouth! That is so disgusting!"

Bradley: "Mom, I am not sticking my tongue in Chico's mouth. He is sticking his in mine."

When Your Lady Is Spoken For

Nate: "Mom, I have bad news for you. I would marry you, but you are already married."

Shower Deliberations

Me (naked and getting out of the shower): "Bradley, you need to get out and let me get dressed in private. You are too old to talk to me when I am naked."

Bradley (10): "Why what's the big deal?"

Me: "It's not a big deal, you are just getting too old."

Bradley: "Does Dad see you naked?"

Me: "Yes, but he is my husband."

Bradley: "Well, I am your son, so what difference does it make? Why can Dad see you naked and I can't?"

Me: "Your dad sees me naked because we are married, and when you are married, your spouse is the only one that gets to see you naked anymore."

Bradley: "Well, that's dumb."

On The Importance of Sunlight

When Bradley was two-years-old, Dave and I hired a babysitter so we could go out to dinner. I was in the bathroom getting ready, and Bradley kept frantically running into the bathroom in a panic, crying and saying, "Mom! You better hurry and go to dinner. It's getting dark outside!" I kept telling him to relax and everything would be okay, but he was getting more and more worked up. Finally, after he ran in for the umpteenth time, I said, "What in the *world* are you so worried about?" He took a deep breath and said in an exasperated tone of voice, "You won't be able to see your food!"

On Being a Ladies Man

Me: "Nate, how was your first day of third grade?"

Nate: "*Horrible*! I am stuck in a girl trap, and I can't get out!"

Me: "What the heck is a *girl trap*?"

Nate: "I have girls sitting *all around me* in the classroom, and *no boys*!"

Me: "Trust me, Nate, someday you will be so happy to be in the girl trap at school."

Nate: "*Never*! And I can't *talk* to any of them because then other kids will think I have a crush on them! So I just sit there staring forward, waiting for them to stop talking to me. I can never talk again."

Who Do You Have a Crush On?

Some family friends were visiting, and their son Jake was driving with us in the car.

Me: "Jake, do you have a girlfriend?"

Jake: "Nope."

Dave: "Are you *sure*, Jake? We won't tell your mom."

Jake: "No, I have never had a girlfriend."

Dave: "Well, do you have a crush on anyone?"

Jake: "Nope."

Nate (piping in): "Why do they call it a 'crush'?"

Me: "Well, they probably call it a crush because it means that you like someone a lot, or even love them, and if they don't love you back, you might feel like your heart was crushed."

Nate: "Well, then I have a crush."

Me: "You do? Who do you have a crush on?"

Nate: 'Daddy."

Bradley's Take on a Crush

Bradley: "Mom, I have a huge crush on you. I am not sure exactly what that means, but I have a crush on you."

Me: "What do you think it means?"

Bradley: "Well, it means that I love you so much that I will share my Star Wars action figures with you."

On Brotherly Love

Bradley: "Mom, let's talk about what I want for my birthday."

Me: "Okay, I know what you want. You want a kiss from your mama."

Bradley: "No, Mom."

Me: "Okay, you want a kiss from your brother."

Bradley: "*No way*, Mom! His kisses are poisonous. He likes girls!"

Me: "Well, you like girls, too."

Bradley: "Yeah, but I only like one girl. Nate likes all girls. He is girl crazy!"

After thinking more about it...

Bradley: "Just so you know, if Nate tries to kiss me, I'm gonna kick him in the balls."

Hallelujah for Confidence!

Bradley (to the girl he has a crush on): "Do you have a crush on anyone?"

Her: "No, do you?"

Bradley: "Yes, I have a crush on you."

On Making Out

Bradley: "Mom, what does it mean to 'make out'?"

Me: "Well, it's kind of like kissing and hugging a lot."

Bradley: "So, you and I *make out* then."

Me: "No, Bradley. You and I don't *make out*. *Making out* is when you kiss and hug for a long time."

Bradley: "Well, we kiss and hug a lot, and sometimes we hug for a long time."

Me: "Bradley. Remember that sex talk we had a few weeks ago? Well, *making out* is closer to sex than it is to hugging."

Bradley: "Eww, I thought I wanted to make out someday, but now, no way."

On Attracting the Ladies

Bradley: "Mom, I noticed something weird lately."

Me: "What is it?"

Bradley: "Some people have hair on their underarms."

Me: "Yep."

Bradley: "Do you have hair on your underarms?"

Me: "I would, but I shave it off."

Bradley: "Does Dad have hair on his underarms?"

Me: "Yes."

Bradley: (panicking and checking) "Do I have hair on my underarms?"

Me: "No, you have to go through puberty first. Then you'll get hair on your underarms."

Bradley: "Thank goodness. I don't think girls would like me if I had hair on my underarms."

On Secret Girlfriends

When Bradley was in fifth grade, we were talking about some of the kids in his class who had girlfriends. I asked him what that meant, and he wasn't entirely sure.

Me: "Do *you* have a girlfriend?"

Bradley: "Yes."

Me: "Do you talk to her or spend time with her?"

Bradley: "No!"

Me: "Well, what do you do? Does she even know that she is your girlfriend?"

Bradley: "No way! One of our friends made the mistake of telling his girlfriend that she was his girlfriend, and now she avoids him. I don't want *that* to happen."

On Love

After waking up, Dave came into the kitchen and gave me a hug and a kiss and said, "Good morning."

Bradley (covering his eyes): "Gross! Tell me when it's over."

Me: "Bradley, don't you want your parents to love each other?"

Bradley: "Yeah, but not in front of me."

Nate: "Yeah, romance burns our eyes!"

Dave: "You sound like your mother."

On Being an Entrepreneur

Nate and I went to the city to renew my business license.

Nate: "Mommy, I need a business license, too."

Me: "Okay, sounds good. What kind of business do you have?"

Nate: "I am in the business of loving you."

The Power of Empathy

I was driving in the car with the kids, and we saw a stray dog.

Me: "Look at that poor dog, he lost his mama."

Bradley: "He isn't lost, Mom. He is traveling the world."

••• 6 •••

Boys and Their Brutal Honesty

On Growing Out of Your Clothes

Me: "Look at that girl with the red and white striped shirt! I have been looking for the same striped shirt so I can be Wenda from Waldo for Halloween next year."

Bradley: "Why would you buy the shirt now? It may not fit you next year when Halloween gets here."

Me: "Adults aren't like kids, Bradley; we don't get bigger every year and grow out of our clothes like kids do."

Bradley: "You do."

Just Like a Marshmallow

Nate and I were snuggling, and he said, "I love snuggling with you because you are soft and squishy like a big cloud."

Time to Get the Roots Done

As I was getting ready to blow dry my hair,

Bradley: "Mom, what is that line on the side of your head?"

Me: "It's called *a part*. You don't have one because your head is shaved."

Bradley: "Well your hair is brown, but your part is white. Is everyone's part like yours?"

Roots, Part 2

Nate (five): "Mom, what's up with those white hairs on your head? All of your hair-dye fell out."

The Benefits of Being Chubby

Dave brought in the mail, and there was a large Weight Watchers postcard on top:

Nate: "Mom, you can't go on Weight Watchers!"

Me: "Why not?"

Nate: "Because I don't want a skinny mom."

Me: "Umm, okay."

Nate: "Plus, when you are chubby, nobody will cannibalize you because nobody will want to eat you because your meat is too fatty and nobody likes all of that fat on their meat."

On Having Wings

The boys and I were snuggling in bed when they decided to use my arms for a zerbert contest.

Nate: "Bradley! Use the fat, squishy, flappy part of Mom's arm—it makes the loudest noise."

Doggie Kisses

Me: "Ah, how cute. The puppy just gave me a kiss on the chin."

Bradley: "Which of your chins did he kiss?"

On Me Getting Old

Nate: "Mom, you should stop wearing makeup, and just accept your fate that you're getting old like a grandma."

Can't a Girl Get a Compliment?

After coming home from getting my hair colored and blown out,

Me: "Boys, you didn't even notice that I got my hair done. Please give me a compliment because that is what you do when a woman gets her hair done."

Bradley: "Nice hair."

Nate: "Nice hair until it turns all grey again and looks weird like usual."

Can't a Girl Get a Compliment? Part 2

After coming home from getting my hair colored,

Nate (looking at me weird): "Mom, you have red in your hair."

Me: "I know. Do you like it?"

Nate: "No."

Me: "Nate, remember when we talked about when a woman gets her hair done, you always need to find *something* nice to say and try to pay her a compliment?"

Nate: "I'm sorry Mom, but there is nothing nice that I can say about your hair."

Heading Straight for AARP

Bradley, pushing my bangs off my face: "Mom, you look like an old granny."

On the Wrinkle Regime

Bradley: "Mom, what's that white stuff you are putting all over your face?"

Me: "It's face cream."

Bradley: "Why are you putting it on your face?"

Me: "For my wrinkles."

Bradley: "You mean those lines all over your face?"

Me: "Yeah, Bradley. That's what I mean."

Bradley: "I like those lines all over your face. It makes you look like a mom."

Dissing Daddy

Nate: "*Mom*! Come look at all of the steam rising off of the fence!"

Bradley: "That's no big deal, Nate. I see that steam come off Dad's bald head all of the time when he goes outside in the cold."

On the Smokey Eye

As I was leaving for work, all made-up and feeling good,

Nate (four) squinting his eyes and tilting his head to the side: "Mom, did someone punch you in the eye?"

I Like Big Butts, and I Cannot Lie

Nate, walking in while I was getting dressed, "Mom, I just saw your big honkin' buns."

Plus-Sized or Pregnant?

Pulling the car into the gas station,

Me: "Look at that poor pregnant lady trying to get gas in the rain."

Bradley: "How do you know she is pregnant?"

Me: "Dude, look at her humongous belly."

Bradley: "Well your belly is humongous, and you aren't pregnant."

I Should Be an Extra in Lord of the Rings

Bradley (six): "Mom, you look like a goblin with that haircut."

Makeup Mystery

Bradley: "Mom, do you have glitter on your eyes?"

Me: "No, my eyeshadow just has some sparkles in it. Do I look pretty?"

Bradley: "No, you look like a monster."

On Speed and Velocity

As Nate and I were getting ready to go down a waterslide in tandem, he yelled to Bradley, who was at the end of a long, crowded line:

"We're gonna *fly* down this slide 'cause Mom weighs a *ton!*"

At Least He's Smart

Nate: "Mom, your hair looks like Albert Einstein."

On Looking Like Groucho Marx

Nate: "Mom, why do you have fuzz all over your top lip? Are girls supposed to have a hairy lip?"

On Too Much Junk in the Trunk

Bradley, after picking out a huge, 50-pound pumpkin at the pumpkin patch,

Bradley: "Mom, we are studying measurements in school, and I want to measure how wide this pumpkin is.

Me: "That sounds like a great idea!"

Bradley (measuring the width of the pumpkin): "Man! This pumpkin is *huge*! Come here, Mom, let me measure your butt. I bet it is bigger than the pumpkin."

Chubby Dancer

Bradley: "Mom, did you have fun at the Zumba convention?"

Me: "Yes, I had a lot of fun!"

Bradley: "Are you going to go again?"

Me: "I don't know. It was fun, but it was expensive, and it's hard to be away from home and work for four days."

Bradley: "I think you should go again."

Me: "Why?"

Bradley: "Well, you are already the *old* Zumba teacher; you don't want to be the old Zumba teacher with old moves.

On Being Cuddly

Me: "Bradley, guess who slept with me last night and kept me awake all night long?"

Bradley: "Chico?"

Me: "Yes, Chico. I thought we got a second dog so he could sleep with *you*. Why is Chico sleeping with *me* every night?"

Bradley: "Because you are big, gushy, soft and warm; it's a dog's dream. No offense."

On Being Attractive

Nate: "Mom, do I have a butt chin?"

Me: "Yes, but it is a called a *cleft* in your chin."

Nate: "It looks horrible!"

Me: "No, it doesn't. Some people even get plastic surgery to get their chin to look like that. It is very attractive!"

Bradley: "I have one, too."

Me (feeling my chin): "Do I have one?"

Bradley: "No. But it doesn't matter because you are married, so even with a cleft in your chin you would be attractive to 0% of the population."

A Compliment—Sort of

Nate: Mom, why do girls wear makeup?"

Me: "To make them look pretty."

Nate: "Does it work?"

Me: "Well, do you think I look pretty with makeup on?"

Nate: "I guess. But I like your face best when we snuggle in the morning."

On Heading Off to Work

Me, heading out the door to work,

Bradley: "Mom, are you looking weird on purpose?"

On Proper Form

Nate (four): "Mom, look at me doing squats like at martial arts class."

Bradley (six): I like to watch Mom squat and put things in the oven because it's funny when her gigantic butt sticks out."

An Alternate Profession

Bradley: "Mom, you have a mustache."

Me: "I know; I'm overdue for a wax. Maybe we can go on a road trip to Ulta, and you can watch me get my lip waxed."

Bradley: "Or you could just let it grow out and join the circus as the bearded lady."

On The Natural Look

Nate: "Mom, do you still have makeup on?"

Me: "Well, what do you think?"

Nate: "Well, I think that you look the same with makeup on as you do with makeup off."

Me: "I'm not sure if that is a good thing or a bad thing. It could mean I am beautiful both ways, or it could mean that I look old and tired both ways."

Nate: "Sorry, Mom, but door number two."

On Not Being Recognized

Bradley: "I think we should all try to be extra healthy this summer and get into really good shape."

Me: "That's a great idea, Bradley. My 25-year high school reunion is this summer, and I need to lose some weight, or nobody will recognize me."

Bradley: "Yeah, they are all going to be like, "Who is that big girl? She's a party crasher."

On Dancing with Your Mom

Me: "Bradley, come slow dance with me to this fun song on the radio."

Bradley (six): "No, thank you."

Me: "Bradley, you need to always dance with a girl when she asks you to dance. And as a son, it is your duty to dance with your mom any time we are at a wedding or special event, and when I want to dance."

Bradley: "Is that a law?"

Me: "Yes, it is a law."

Bradley: "I'd rather go to jail."

Get Me a Duck Call

As the boys snuggled into bed with me and the sunlight streamed into the bedroom,

Nate: "Mom, how come you are a girl, and you have a beard?"

Me: "I don't have a beard! It's just the sun shining through the window that makes it look like that."

Bradley: "I can see the beard, too. You look like the guys on *Duck Dynasty*."

On Being XL

While folding clean clothes with the boys, Bradley picked up a pair of my sweats and said, "I hope these aren't mine because if they are, I've gotten really fat."

Mama Needs Some Botox

Lying in bed with Nate (six) reading a bedtime story:

Nate: "Mom, what is that weird smell?"

Me: "It is my lotion that I put on my face to make my skin look nice and get rid of my wrinkles."

Nate: "Sorry, Mom, but now you smell weird, and I can still see your wrinkles."

On Carrying Some Extra Poundage

The family was watching the reality show *Survivor* on TV, and the contestants had a challenge where their family members came to visit and compete with them.

Bradley: "If I went on *Survivor,* nobody in my family could help me because everyone is out of shape."

Reflections from Mom

Alright, please excuse me while I bandage up my self-esteem after that last section. I love my sons to the moon and back, but when they were younger and would share that top-of-the-mind thinking on a regular basis, sometimes it felt a little brutal. Even though my jaw dropped during some of these comments, I always knew deep down that they adored me, and I still believe it.

As my boys got older, they learned how to handle themselves with more maturity and restraint than when they were younger. Now my boys regularly find something nice to say when I come home from the hair salon and my hair is a different color than when I left. Even when they don't like their food at dinner (at my house or somebody else's house), they smile, eat what is served to them, and say thank you.

In my house, this is the huge payoff; the boys having the wisdom to know when they should be upfront and honest, and when they should engage in a white lie to spare someone's heart and feelings. In the end, isn't this what a relationship is all about?

PART III

LIFE

LIFE IS A beautiful thing. For a growing child, learning about life and how the world works is inevitable. As Bradley and Nate started learning about the world around them, they often had funny questions and observations about everything from what puberty is, to how language is created, to why we celebrate holidays, to everyday responsibilities. Essentially, they had questions about life.

In fact, as each of us was growing up, we had to learn about language. We had to learn that words carried weight and that words can sometimes be confusing. As we got older and were developing our vocabularies, we sometimes had questions about what words meant and how to use them. As for kids, occasionally they misinterpret words and language, which can be just plain funny.

Young kids also start to earn an allowance, and they definitely begin to learn about their parents' jobs, life responsibilities, and sometimes even death. It's interesting to see the world through a child's eyes and to learn how they view jobs and working. I remember when I was a small child and wanted something, I would tell my mom to write a check. As a kid, I did not understand that a check was actually tied to a bank account that either had money in it or it didn't. My kids went through this same phase when they would say, "Just use your ATM card to buy it!"

I distinctly remember talking to my boys about hygiene as well. Man, can boys get stinky! We talked a lot about using deodorant, washing and scrubbing their hair and showering every day. I continue to battle with them about showering daily and frequent haircuts.

Each time I take the boys to get their haircut, it is an all-out war because they hate getting their hair cut. Every five weeks or so, when we must get it done, I have to explain the importance of taking care of their body and presenting themselves in the best way possible. It is especially difficult for me to get Bradley on board, so I carefully sneak in a stop at the hair salon on the way home from somewhere else. He usually won't talk to me for at least half an hour after it is over. But at least he doesn't look like a Q-tip anymore.

··· 7 ···

Teaching Boys Responsibility

When Dad Takes Care of the Toddler

WHEN YOU LEAVE your children at home with their dad and go out of town, sometimes things can go awry. Let me preface this by saying when I started this whole parenting thing, I was one of those moms who would freak out about every detail: they had to eat the right foods, sleep on the right schedule, listen to the right books, and wear the right clothes. Anytime I left town, I stressed so much about things being done *wrong* while I was gone that I just couldn't enjoy myself.

Until one day, I talked to one of my girlfriends who said, "You know, as long as the kids are alive when I get home, I don't stress about all of the other stuff." The more I thought about it, the more I realized that I was causing myself too much stress. So, from then on, I didn't care if they wore plaid shorts with a striped shirt when dad was in control. I didn't care if they ate cereal for dinner, and I didn't care if their diaper soaked through in the middle of the night because dad didn't put it on tight enough. As long as they were alive when I got home, I learned to be content with whatever happened while I was gone. Once I freed myself from this worry, my life was much happier.

One particular day when Bradley was about three or four years old, I left him home with Dave while I went out for a few hours to run errands. I came home just after lunchtime, and Dave announced proudly, "This boy sure loves milk!" "What do you mean?" I asked, looking at the empty half-gallon milk container sitting on the counter. "He drank that whole thing."

The next scene came straight out of a horror movie: As I was turning to look at Bradley while saying, "Nooooooooo........" in what seemed like slow motion, Bradley stared at me with a funny look on his face and proceeded to throw up the half gallon of milk all over the kitchen counter. I looked at Dave, shaking my head, and he shrugged and said, "Lesson learned."

Catching a Virus

Me: "Boys, I wish you could come into my college class and sit and learn and watch me teach."

Nate: "No way! Just my luck, I would catch puberty from all of those teenagers."

Deodorant Options

Nate (smelling his armpits, then mine): "Mom, how come your armpits smell like roses when mine are stinky?"

Me: "Well, I use deodorant, Nate. It hides the stink and makes it smell nice. Maybe we should get some for you."

Nate: "I don't want to smell like roses. Do they have boy smelling deodorant like muscles and baseball?"

Cleaning More Than Plaque

I heard Bradley (six) groaning and moaning from the bathroom and thought, "*Well, this should be interesting.*" I hesitantly peeked around the corner to find him scratching his back with his electric toothbrush. I wonder how long *that* has been going on.

On Understanding How Life Works

Nate: "Mom, I am glad you make me and Bradley work for things because nothing in life is free."

Me: "Yep. It's important to work hard for things. But I can think of one thing in life that is free."

Nate: "Wait! Me too!"

Me: "Ah, Nate. You and I are thinking the same thing; I was thinking that love is free."

Nate: "I wasn't thinking that love is free, Mom. I was thinking that apps are free."

On Not Looking Like a Slob

Me: "Nate, you have your basketball banquet coming up. Coach says you have to wear a shirt and tie."

Nate (sighing): "This is like what I am going to have to do when I get drafted by the NBA."

Me: "Um. Sure; okay."

Nate: "Can I wear my Golden State Warriors t-shirt and a tie?"

Me: "No, you have to wear a button-down shirt, like a nice shirt."

Nate: "My t-shirt is a nice shirt. It's an expensive one."

Being Hot in a Bad Way

Nate: "Mom, why are you putting that fan by your bed?"

Me: "I am starting to go through menopause, and I get hot in the middle of the night."

Bradley: "What is menopause?"

Nate: "Duh. It is when puberty ends, and you feel hot in a bad way, not the good hot you feel in puberty."

On Eating Vegetables

Bradley: "Mom, I found out today that I actually *do* eat plants and vegetables."

Me: "How is that, Bradley?"

Bradley: "Well, I learned that garlic is a bulb and grows in the ground, right?"

Me: "Well, yes, it does grow in the ground, I guess."

Bradley: "And I like to eat lots of garlic bread, so therefore, I eat my vegetables."

Someone Is Going to Get a Time-Out

Me: "Bradley, you *have* to take a bath tonight!"

Bradley: "*Why?* I don't want to take a bath!"

Me: "Because you *stink*, that's why!"

Bradley: "Well, you *stink* as a parent!"

At Least He is Tidy

After sending Bradley into the bathroom to brush his teeth, I found him *scrubbing the sink* with his electric toothbrush.

Me: "Dude. What the heck are you doing? People spit in there; it's totally germy."

Bradley: "What's the big deal, Mom, I have done this my whole life."

Great.

On Facing the Music

Me: "Nate, we have your parent-teacher conference tomorrow, and we both have to go."

Nate: "I don't want to go."

Me: "Why don't you want to go?"

Nate: "I'd rather just have her talk about me behind my back."

On Not Being Able to Eat

Nate (dealing with his first loose tooth): "My tooth is loose, and my chompers aren't working."

Me: "Do you want me to pull it out so you can eat?"

Nate: "Yes, please."

So, I reached over, pinched his tooth between my fingers, and yanked it right out. He put a towel on it for a second, and then smiled and ate his breakfast.

#boys

Bradley, Passing Knowledge on to his Brother...

After Nate's loose tooth *finally* came out,

Bradley: "Nate! You scored the jackpot! You lost your tooth on the last day of the month, and you *know* the tooth fairy gets paid on the first of every month. So, when she comes tomorrow, you are gonna get lots of money!"

On Getting Ready for Leadership

Nate: "I was thinking about running for sixth-grade class president, but I changed my mind."

Dave: "Dude, go for it! Girls always love the class president!"

Nate: "Eww! Then I'm going to wait until after I start puberty to run for class president—like maybe in high school."

On Running out of Toothpaste

Bradley (yelling from the bathroom): "Mom! We are out of kid's toothpaste!"

Me: "Just use mine."

Bradley: "Okay."

About 10 seconds later...

Bradley: "Mom! This tastes really gross and weird!"

Me: "What are you using? What does it say on the tube?"

Bradley: "It says, A and D Diaper Rash Ointment."

It's All in What You Call It

Bradley: "Mom, what's for dinner?"

Me (combining ground turkey, refried beans, and cheese in a pan): "Quesadillas."

Bradley: "We hate those quesadillas. They are so gross."

Me (secretly taking the mixture I just created and sticking it in a bowl instead of a tortilla): "I meant we are having Mexican chili for dinner."

Bradley: "We love Mexican chili!"

#winning

Failing at Being Cool

Nate, getting dressed for preschool, sitting and sniffling in the corner of his room:

Me: What's wrong, baby?"

Nate: "Mom, there's a turtle on my shirt."

Me: "I know. That shirt is so adorable."

Nate: "Mom, turtles aren't cool."

··· 8 ···

How We Learn Language

A Twist on Words

WHEN NATE WAS about six, he was bitten by a dog in the face and required stitches. I worried about Nate sitting still when they numbed and stitched his face. I didn't want to take any risks putting him under anesthesia, so on the way to the ER, I kept telling Nate, "Let's try really hard to sit still while they do the stitches, so they don't have to put you to sleep. If we can avoid putting you to sleep, that would be ideal."

Nate looked at me wide-eyed, and said, "Okay, Mom, I will sit still."

Of course, after we got there, and there were three nurses and a doctor with a huge needle hovering over him, and me laying my entire body on him to keep him still, Nate would have no part of it. We tried and tried to get him to sit still to numb the area, but no-can-do. Finally, I said to the doctor, "Okay, you are going to have to put him to sleep; this is just too traumatic for him." Nate started crying and hysterically shouting, "I can do it, Mom; I can do it! Please don't put me to sleep!" I couldn't figure out why he was so panicked about being put to sleep, until he cried out, "I don't want to die!"

And then, I remembered. One of our neighbors had to "put their dog to sleep" a few weeks earlier, so Nate thought we were going to *put him to sleep*…permanently. Parent of the Year move right there.

Smarty Pants

Me: "Bradley, you peed all over your pants. What the heck is wrong with you?"

Bradley: "What's the big deal? It's just my underwear?"

Me: "Dude. You're walking around with piss pants."

Nate: "Mom, you just used alliteration with bad words."

He's Hard Core

Bradley, looking over my shoulder while I was checking my email, and seeing an email from a girl who wanted to add my class at the college where I teach:

Bradley: "Mom, are you going to let that girl add your class?"

Me: "I don't know, do you think I should?"

Bradley: "No."

Me: "Why not?"

Bradley: "In her email, she has two spelling errors and two words that should be capitalized but aren't. Don't add her. She needs to figure things out."

Saving for a Rainy Day

While on a bike ride,

Bradley: "Mom, can we go around the cul-de-sac?"

Me: "Sure."

Nate: "Will there really be a sack of gold there?"

Me: "What are you talking about, Nate? Why would there be gold there?"

Nate: "We are going on the *gold sack*, aren't we? Do we have to split the gold or can I have it all?"

On Being Wordy

Bradley (nine) writing his three-paragraph book report,

Me: "Bradley, you have more than three paragraphs. Is that okay?"

Bradley: "Mom, I'm not the kind of kid who can say things in just three paragraphs. I have lots to say."

Everyone Loves Cake

We bought a Bundt cake at Trader Joe's, and when we opened it at home, Nate gasped and said, "It has a hole in the middle!"

Me: "It's a *Bundt* cake."

Nate: "A *butt* cake? I am not eating a *butt* cake! No way!"

Me (over-enunciating): "Not *butt*, Nate. *Bundt, Bundt.*"

Nate (looking puzzled, still not understanding) "Whatever, Mom. As long as it has cinnamon on top, I'll eat the butt cake."

On Repeating What They Hear

Me: "Boys, you need to get in the shower."

Nate: "Mom, don't have a hernia."

Nate (whispers to Bradley): "What's a *hernia?*"

On Bee Behavior

Me (as a bee was flying around us): "Nate, don't freak out over the bee. It doesn't want to sting you; it knows it will die if it stings you, so just be cool."

Nate: "But I don't want to get stung."

Me: "Seriously, it is not the end of the world if you get stung."

Nate: "It is for the bee."

No Name-Calling

Bradley: "Mom, there is a totally mean and inappropriate show on TV called *The Biggest Loser*. It's not okay to call someone a *loser*. That show should not be on TV."

When Spelling Backfires

When the boys were little, there were certain words that we would spell when we were talking. "Fat" was one of them. I didn't want the boys calling people fat, or someday worrying that they were fat, so we always spelled out that word.

One day, my mom and I took the boys to a little local farm (designed for kids). I asked my mom, "Will you put my ATM card in your purse so I don't have to take my wallet?" Of course, she said yes, and when we got up to the front of the line to pay, Bradley looked at the cashier and said, "My grandma is holding my mom's F-A-T card."

Spelling Challenges

Bradley: "Mom, have you ever seen how people spell *quesadilla*?" Why in the world would they spell it that way? No wonder I can't spell."

#kindatrue

On Dumb Robots

The boys and I were watching *Teenage Mutant Ninja Turtles*, and Bradley looked at me and said, "I don't like that robot guy on there. He always speaks using run-on sentences."

You Gotta Be You

Me (telling Bradley a story): "Remember that time when you were sitting by the fence and (blah blah blah)?"

Bradley (shaking his head no): "Mom, that doesn't ring the doorbell."

Me: "You mean, *ring a bell*."

Bradley: "No, I like saying it doesn't ring the doorbell better, so that is how I am going to say it."

On Being Philosophical

Nate (four) on the morning after a sleepover, where he got up at 5 am,

Nate: "Mom, I drank in the sunrise this morning."

Me (thinking he had some divine intervention and wisdom beyond his years): "Sweetie, that is so amazing."

Nate: "It *was* amazing. I just love that drink that is supposed to be juice, but is really junk."

Me: "Ooh, you mean Sunny D."

Nate: "Yea, that's the one. It's so good."

On Newborn Terminology

When Bradley was four-years-old, he loved to sit and look at the photo album of when Nate was born and stayed in the NICU. He would always say, "Can we sit down and look at the pictures of when Nate hatched?"

On Being Normal

We were eating breakfast as a family, and Bradley (seven) looked at all of us and said, "I have been thinking; I just want to say that I am the only one in this entire family who is not a nut case."

Me: "Think again."

At Least He is Smart

Bradley: "Mom, can you make me an after-school snack, please?"

After I made a little plate of apples, peanut butter, crackers, nuts, and one animal cookie:

Bradley: "Can I just eat the animal cookie? All I wanted was some sugar."

Me: "Bradley! Quit wasting my time if you didn't want the snack to begin with. It's not like I don't have five million other things to be doing or anything."

Nate: "Mom, you just used a hyperbole."

Drinking vs. Eating

Me: "Why are you eating pretzels right before dinner?"

Bradley: "I need a hangover."

Me: "What are you talking about?"

Bradley: "You know, a hangover. Something to hang me over until dinner."

Me: "You mean something to *tide you over* until dinner."

Bradley: "A hangover, a tideover, whatever works so I can have a snack."

On Being an Angry Mom

Nate (five): "Are you one of those angry moms who chase people and try to kill them?"

Me: "What? What are you talking about?"

And after much questioning, he was talking about an *angry mob*, but got confused and thought it was a group of angry moms chasing people with rakes and stuff, trying to kill people.

On Expressing Emotion Correctly

Bradley (four): "Mom, I am so bummed."

Me: "What's the matter?"

Bradley: "I am just bummed."

He kept saying over and over again, until finally...

Bradley: "Mom, what does *bummed* mean?"

I Intercepted That One

It was Scrabble Day at the boys' school, and they were supposed to use duct tape to make a letter on the front of their shirts. Then, they were to go to school and find friends with different letters and make words. I loved this idea *until* Bradley came out of his room cracking up. He decided to take it one step further; he put a *U* on his shirt, then two *T*'s on his crotch to stand for each testicle and a *B* on his rear end to spell out *butt*.

Too Cute to Get into Trouble

Nate's preschool teacher (when he was acting up during nap time): "Nate, stop misbehaving. Do you want me to tell your mom that you weren't following directions at nap time?"

Nate: "No, just tell her that I love her."

... 9 ...

Managing Holidays and Other Important Days

On Asking the Magic 8 Ball a Few Questions on Christmas Eve

Nate (shaking the Magic 8 Ball): "Does Santa think Nate is a good boy?"

The Magic 8 Ball: "My sources say no."

Nate (in a panic, shaking the Magic 8 Ball again): "Is Nate going to get coal in his stocking tonight?"

Nate (reading the Magic 8 Ball response): "Without a doubt."

Nate: "*Mom*! The Magic 8 Ball says Santa's going to bring me coal!"

Me: "You know, Nate, if you clean your room and do some chores, I am sure the Magic 8 Ball would change its mind."

Nate (running off to clean his room): "On it!"

Dave (to me): "Good one."

Everyone Should Recycle

Bradley: "Mom! Thanks for the little bag of chocolate gold coins for St. Patrick's Day!"

Me: "You're welcome, sweetheart."

Bradley (after opening one and popping it in his mouth): "Mom! These chocolates are all old and gross. Wait a minute. Are these the same gold chocolate coins that you gave us last year for St. Patrick's Day?"

#fail

On Picking the Right Outfit for Picture Day

When Bradley was in kindergarten, he was so excited for his first school picture day. I told him to go into his bedroom and pick out a perfect outfit; an outfit that made him happy. He excitedly ran into his bedroom, and a few minutes later emerged in the sweetest outfit I had ever seen: His favorite pajama top, covered by his favorite tank top, and a clip-on "special occasion" tie. To this day, this is my favorite school picture outfit he has ever worn.

On Free Christmas Presents

Bradley: "Mom, I know what I want for Christmas. It might be a little hard to get, but it is *free!*"

Me: "Wow, Bradley. I am liking this! What is it?"

Bradley: "I want a baseball signed by all of the Dodgers."

Me: "Hmm...well, that would be pretty impossible to get, Bradley. How about we buy a baseball and Dad and I will sign all of the Dodgers names on it?"

Bradley: "Sounds good to me!"

#HomeRun!

Scared of Ghosts

When Bradley and Nate were four- and six-years-old, we were lying in bed reading books and telling stories about Halloween. Out of nowhere the doorbell rang, and Nate went to look through the window to see who it was. He immediately ran back to the bedroom, hysterically crying and screaming, "There's a ghost in our front yard!"

By the sheer look of terror on his face, I thought for a second there might actually be a ghost in our front yard. I hesitantly walked down the hallway, peeking around the corner to see what was going on. I was freaked out, the boys were crying, and Dave was out of town. I thought to myself, "Get it together, woman! Go look and see if there is a ghost out there!"

I slowly walked through the living room, my hand shaking as I pulled back the curtain so I could peek out into the front yard. That's when I saw it—a four-foot-tall white, stuffed, kiddie ghost decoration standing right in front of our front door.

Laughing, I opened the door to see two of our sweet neighbors hiding behind my car, trying to contain their hysterics. They had bought the stuffed ghost as a gift for the boys, and although they felt horrible that it had scared the bejeezus out of them, they thought the whole scenario was hilarious.

I brought the ghost inside to show Bradley and Nate, but they still weren't very happy about it. They understood it wasn't real, but they were still scared of it. They allowed me to leave the ghost out as a Halloween decoration in our living room, but they made me turn the ghost around backwards so they couldn't see its face.

Bradley and Nate lived with the ghost in the living room through Halloween, but on the morning of November 1, when I came groggily walking down the hallway to get coffee, I heard a strange noise coming from the front room. It sounded like loud grunting. I came around the corner to find Nate on top of the ghost, punching it as hard as he could in the face, knocking its head off. Poor thing; he was so traumatized by that ghost. But I guess in the end, he showed it who was boss.

On Not Getting Sucked into Relationship Drama

Me: "Nate, are you going to give a valentine to any special girls tomorrow?"

Nate: "No! One of our class rules on the board is 'no drama' with *three* underlines. Giving Valentine's gifts just creates drama, and I don't want to get into trouble."

On Staying on Santa's Nice List

Nate (four) wrestling with Bradley, yelled: "Get your finger out of my butt or Santa won't bring you presents!"

On Shopping for a Present to Take to a Girl's Birthday Party

Nate: "Mom, we need to go to the yucky *girl* store to buy her a present."

Me: "What do you think they sell at the yucky girl store?"

Nate: "You know, boobs, skinny eyebrows, poufy hair, mommies, girl beds with mermaids on them—all of the yucky girl stuff."

On Dog Toys

We came home from a fun day to find that Chico had torn apart a big, stuffed Santa decoration that we had in the living room.

Bradley: "*Oh no*, Mom! Chico murdered Santa!"

On Being Stubborn

When Bradley was five, he wanted to be a Power Ranger for Halloween. We got his costume at the beginning of October, and he played in it every day. He loved that costume. When the evening of October 31st finally rolled around, I went into his bedroom and said, "Bradley, let's put on your costume so we can go around the block trick-or-treating!" He just looked at me and said, "No."

I tried and tried to coax him into putting it on. I mean, seriously, he had worn that costume every day for a month! But unfortunately, he would have no part of it. He wanted to go trick-or-treating, he just didn't want to wear the costume. So that year, he ended up going trick-or-treating in his jeans and a grey sweatshirt, as The Kid Who Refuses to Wear His Costume. The neighbors got a kick out of it.

Trick-Or-Treating Excitement

Bradley: "That lady just gave us a full-sized candy bar! I was so excited that I accidentally just peed a little in my costume."

Mom Nags

Bradley: "I know what I want to be when I grow up."

Me: "Ooh, really. What?"

Bradley: "I want to be Santa Claus. Then I would get to eat pounds and pounds of cookies without you always bossing me around and telling me that I can only have one."

Prince or Princess?

Nate: "Mom, what if Santa gets confused and brings me those girl Legos, Lego Friends?"

Me: "Nate, Santa won't get confused, I promise."

Nate: "But what if he does? All of my friends will make fun of me if I get Princess Legos!"

Me: "Really, Nate. Santa is super organized. You don't need to worry."

Nate: (whispering in my ear so Bradley won't hear) "Okay, Mom. If Santa brings me Princess Legos, I will just set up a secret play area that is hidden and play with them in there."

#ThinkingHeSecretlyWantsPrincessLegos

Halloween Dud

Me: "Boys, let's go to the pumpkin patch and get some fun pumpkins to carve for Halloween. Then, we can take a cute fall picture sitting on the pumpkins like all of the other fun families."

Both boys: "Can't you just go to Trader Joe's and get pumpkins there?"

'Tis the season...for grumps.

On Bribing Saint Nick

I took the boys to get their Santa pictures, and as we were driving there, I noticed Bradley (six) had some coins in his hand.

Me: "Bradley, what are you doing with that money?"

Bradley: "I took some money out of my piggy bank to slip to Santa so he won't put me on the naughty list."

Negotiating with Neighbors on Halloween

On Halloween night, we took the boys trick or treating around the block. Bradley (four) was given a Mounds bar from one of our distant neighbors. Bradley picked the Mounds bar out of his bag, looked at it, and in his best salesman voice said, "I'll trade you back this Mounds bar, plus two hard candies and this box of crayons for that Reese's peanut butter cup in your bowl."

#Let'sMakeABadDeal

Santa Screw Up

Nate: "Mom, it is so windy outside, and I am worried that Santa is going to get blown off track and deliver my presents to Taiwan."

High Career Aspirations

Bradley (five): "Mom, what is a *job*?"

Me: "It is when adults go to work to make money to support themselves and their families, and when you pick a job, you want one that makes you happy and fills your heart with joy."

Bradley (after thinking about it for 20 minutes): "Mom, I have been thinking about what you said, and I know what I want to do for my job when I get older. I want to be a professional trick-or-treater."

Being a Rule-Follower

Nate: "Mom, does Santa Claus have to go through customs?"

That Was a Close One

Nate (four) sitting around the dinner table with family and friends on Christmas Eve: "I have a riddle!"

Everybody stopped and gave him their full attention.

Nate: "What word starts with an 'F' and ends with 'uck'?"

After what seemed like the most awkward silence in history.

Nate: "Firetruck!"

We all just about died.

The Tooth Fairy's Budgeting Skills

When Bradley lost his first tooth, the tooth fairy left him $5.00.

After waking up and finding the loot: "Mom! The tooth fairy left me $5.00, and she only gave $1.00 to some of my friends at school! She must have just gotten her paycheck and had some extra money."

And when Nate lost his first tooth...

Nate (after losing his first tooth): "Mom, how much money do you think the tooth fairy will leave me for my tooth?"

Bradley: "Well, it depends if she just got paid or not. Depending on the day of the month, she could give you $20, or she could give you a quarter."

Nate (visibly worried): Well, when does she get paid? It's the end of the month!"

Bradley: She gets paid at the beginning of the month. It looks like you are going to get duped."

#brotherlylove

Liar, Liar, Pants on Fire

The boys were driving me crazy about watching TV while on Christmas break.

Bradley (six): "Mom, my kindergarten teacher said that we have to watch a lot of TV on our break for 'educational purposes.'"

Me: "Really? You know that I can call your teacher *and* that Santa is listening to what you are saying right now."

Bradley (with a horrified look on his face): "Well maybe those weren't her *exact* words."

A No-Brainer Halloween Costume

Me: "Guess what I ordered yesterday?"

Nate: "My Halloween costume?"

Me: "Yes!"

Dave: "Nate, What are you going to be for Halloween?"

Nate: "A T. rex."

Dave: "A T. rex? Why a T. rex? Isn't that kind of babyish?"

Nate: "It is a blow-up costume, and there is a fan that blows in the pants to keep the costume poufy, so basically, it will fan my junk all night."

Dave: "We all need a T. Rex Costume!"

Reflections from Mom

Over the years, these discussions about life made me realize just how much Bradley and Nate were growing up. Now that they are older, they still ask all kinds of questions about life; however, nothing can replace these exploratory years, when they were just learning about responsibilities, holidays, and building their vocabularies.

PART IV

IMAGINATION

LITTLE BOYS (AND sometimes even big boys) often live in a fantasy world. Whether that fantasy world includes pirates, robots, or video games, most boys love to live in a world of make believe. Many prominent researchers in the field of psychology make the case that imaginative or pretend play helps kids develop creativity, social skills, empathy, cooperation, negotiation skills, and more.[5] People who interact with kids on a regular basis most likely already realize that stoking the fire of a child's imagination can lead to amazing results. When you watch little boys play, there is a certain element of being carefree that is to be envied.

Little boys also have extraordinarily vivid imaginations, but sometimes they use their imaginations to test boundaries and limits. They can pick up bad habits and bad words from inside and often outside the home. They may start using swear words (even when they don't know what they mean), name-call, break rules, and more. They may also attempt to assert dominance over each other, and sometimes even over their parents. Whether it is asking questions about drugs, or learning about swear words for the first time, boys like to test boundaries.

••• 10 •••

Boys and Their Carefree Ways

The Portal in Nate's Closet

WHEN NATE WAS about three-years-old, he went through a stage where he went into his bedroom, sat in the dark closet and had conversations. I thought that he had an imaginary friend, and initially, it was sweet. Then, he started to do it more and more, and I could hear full-on conversations going on when he was behind the closed closet door.

After a while, I started to worry that something funny was going on, and I convinced myself that he was speaking to someone "on the other side" and that maybe his closet was a portal to the beyond. Every time I would ask Nate who he was talking to, he always said, "The Messenger." The Messenger? This person had a formal name? I was scared shitless. "Who is The Messenger? What does The Messenger say?" I would ask Nate over and over again. He always answered with vague replies, and would just say that he liked talking to her.

This went on for a couple of weeks, and I had enough. Nate always asked for me to leave him alone when he went into the closet to talk to The Messenger, but screw that. He was in the middle of a conversation with *her* when I burst open the closet door. He looked at me, smiled, and held out our cordless landline phone to me, shrieking, "Here! Talk to the Messenger!"

I took the phone from his hand and was petrified as to what I would hear on the other end. I slowly raised the phone to my ear and listened. It was the recording of the operator repeating, "You have dialed a number that is incorrect. Please try again." For weeks, Nate had been sneaking the phone into the closet to dial random numbers so he could get the operator's recording and have a conversation with her. I was just relieved that we didn't in fact have a portal to the other side in Nate's room.

On Cheering for the U.S. Olympians on TV

Bradley and Nate (emphatically yelling and cheering): "*Come on, USA! We believe in you! You can do it!*"

Dave (laughing): "How come you boys couldn't cheer for your rookie baseball teammates this year in the same way that you are cheering for the Olympic volleyball players?"

Nate: "It's not the same, Dad."

Dave: "Yeah, you both spent your time in the dugout completely oblivious to what your team was doing, wrestling and kicking the crap out of each other. Remember that? Why weren't you cheering them on like you are now?"

Bradley: "Because this team may actually win."

Let's Party!

Me (while folding clothes): "Boys! Come help me fold socks; we can have a sock-folding party!"

Bradley: "That's not a party. A party is supposed to be fun."

Me: "It is fun! See the big pile of clean socks that I spread out? It is kind of like that game we used to play called Memory. Do you remember that game?"

Bradley: If the Memory game means finding matches and folding socks until we die of boredom, then, unfortunately, I have played it before."

On Taking Soccer Seriously

Dave: "Nate, are you going to screw around and dance on the soccer field like you did at the game last week, or are you going to play soccer at your game today?"

Nate: (very seriously): "Duh, Dad. I am going to dance."

On Who Should Host the Olympics

Bradley (eight): "Mom, I have the best idea *ever* for how a country can win the bid to host the Olympics!"

Me: "Really? What's your idea?"

Bradley: "They should have all of the athletes stuff their pants with candy, and at the end of each of their competitions, the candy would spill out of their pants onto the floor for everyone to eat! Whoever has the best candy gets to host the Olympics!"

Be Proud, California

We were talking to Bradley and Nate about our upcoming trip to Disneyland and California Adventure.

Me: "I am excited to go on the ride Flying over California when we go to California Adventure."

Nate: "Why?"

Me: "Well, many of the people who go to these parks are not from California, so it is special for them to see all of the cool California things that we get to enjoy every day. On the ride, people get to see the beautiful coastline of California, the strawberry fields, and all of the other special things that make California a wonderful place to live."

Nate: "Do you fly over Domino's Pizza on that ride? Because that's the best part of California."

Can't We All Be in the Olympics?

On the night before the Olympics started,

Bradley (eight): "Is Aunt Teri competing in the Olympics?"

Me (laughing): "No, she is *going* to the Olympics, not competing. What sport did you think she was competing in?"

Bradley: "Swimming. She is a pretty good swimmer. Dangit; I wanted to watch her on TV."

On Time Travel

Nate: "Mom, I want to tell you something, but I am scared to tell you."

Me: "Nate, never be scared to tell me things."

Nate (hesitantly): "Are you sure?"

Me: "Absolutely."

Nate: "Okay. Here it is: I can time travel."

Me: (trying not to laugh): "How do you know that you can time travel?"

Nate: "Well, I woke up this morning and looked at the clock and it said 5:30 and then I closed my eyes and opened them again, and it said 6:45. Mom, I went into the future."

The Protector

Describing our dog in the *I Spy* Game:

Me: "I spy, something with my little eye that is yellowish-white, protects you, and has tons of hair."

Nate: "Jesus?"

The Joy of Playing "I Spy" (2)

Me (describing an inner tube while we were at the water park): "I spy, something with my little eye that is big, round and moves when you push it."

Nate: "Your belly?"

It's Only Fair

Bradley (seven): Mom, when are we going to win the lottery? We have been buying tickets for so long. It's our turn to win!"

••• 11 •••

When Boys Test Limits

ALL PARENTS MAKE mistakes with their first child, and generally speaking, we learn from our errors and do better the second time around. Bradley and his sleeping scenario was no exception. We had gotten in the habit of putting Bradley to sleep by giving him a bottle, snuggling, and rocking him to sleep. It got to a point where he couldn't go to sleep without this ritual.

When Bradley was about two-years-old, we were trying to break him of the habit of being rocked to sleep every night. So, we would give him big hugs and kisses, and lie him down in his crib. Without fail, he would pop right back up to a standing position, look at Dave or me, stick his finger down his throat, and throw up the entire contents of his stomach.

He was manipulating us when he didn't want to go to bed, because he knew by throwing up everywhere, that he would get a nice warm bath, clean sheets, and snuggles. Dave and I got so frustrated with this recurring nightmare that we went to our pediatrician's office to get some expert advice. He took one look at us, laughed, and said, "That boy has you exactly where he wants you."

He then suggested that the next time Bradley did it, to just leave him in his crib and let him sleep in the vomit. I looked at Bradley's doctor like he was out of his mind; there was no way in hell that I was going to let my kid sleep in a crib filled with vomit, while also being covered in vomit. But after some coaxing, Dave and I agreed to try it.

That night, in Bradley's predictable form, he did it. He purposely threw up all over himself to try to get to stay up longer with us. Dave and I just looked at him, told him we loved him, turned off the light, and listened to that kid scream for at least an hour. That was the longest hour of my life. After he finally fell asleep, Dave and I tag teamed and went into

Bradley's bedroom to gently lift him up, change the sheets, and do our best to clean him up a little. Letting him sleep in that mess was terribly hard to do; but man, that kid never, ever did that again. Problem solved.

First Day of School

Bradley: "The best thing about starting school tomorrow is being away from Nate for six hours and five minutes every day."

On Kids Thinking Outside of the Box

My boys came to me one day asking tons of questions about the "f-bomb" and "flipping the bird." I explained what they were, but said that they were not appropriate to say or do. Later, I heard fits of laughter coming from their room, and walked in to find them flipping each other off with their middle toes.

Figuring Out the Good Swear Words

Nate: "*Mom*! Isaac said the 'f-bomb' at preschool."

Me: "He did? Are you sure?"

Nate: "*Yes, I am sure*! I don't know what the 'f-bomb' is, but he said it!"

A few minutes later, Nate comes back into the room:

Nate: "Mom, is *shit* the f-bomb?"

Me: "No."

Nate: "Is *damn* the f-bomb?"

Me: "No."

Nate: "Is *ass* the f-bomb?"

Me: "Nate! Stop saying those words!"

Nate, continuing to pester me about it until finally,

Me: "Stop it, Nate! The *f-bomb* is *fuck*, okay!"

Nate (after a long pause): "Well who cares about *that* word?"

I Guess We Need to Go Shopping

Bradley: "Mom! Nate called me an 'a-word!'"

Me: "Nate. You are too young to use words like that. I need my boys to have some class. Can you try to have some class?"

Bradley: "Sorry to break it to you, Mom. We can't have class if we don't have a tuxedo."

Back-Talker

Me: "Bradley, you need to clean up your room."

Bradley (five): "Plug your pie-hole, Mom."

Me, red-faced and angry: "You did *not* just say that to me!"

Bradley (crying): "What? What? What does it mean?"

Someone Needs Space

Bradley: "So, it looks pretty official—the sixth graders are going to the waterpark to celebrate graduation. This flyer says the whole family can get in for $10; however, I would prefer that my whole family stay home."

Trying to Protect the Loot

When Bradley was about three-years-old, he was obsessed with Dora the Explorer, and more specifically, Swiper the Fox. Swiper was always getting in trouble for stealing things, and one of the catchphrases in the show was, "Swiper! No Swiping!"

Bradley loved to go around saying, "Swiper! No Swiping." And he always pretended to be looking for Swiper. One day I was doing some cooking, and I took off my wedding ring so I could hand mix some ingredients. When I was finished (many hours later), I looked, and my wedding ring was gone. I looked everywhere, and asked both of the boys if they had seen my ring."

Bradley had a sly look on his face, and said, "I hide it."

Me: "Why did you hide it? Where is it?"

Bradley: "I hided it from Swiper because I don't want him to swipe it."

Me: "Well, where did you hide it? That is a special ring, and mama needs it back."

Bradley: "I can't remember."

And he really couldn't remember. We looked *everywhere* for my ring, and I was convinced that he flushed it down the toilet or something similar. Months went by and still no ring. Bradley was convinced that Swiper had shown up and stolen it.

I had pretty much given up on ever finding my ring, until one day, I was cleaning out a drawer in the bathroom, and in the very back corner of the drawer, I found my ring! I showed Bradley where it was, and he had a huge grin on his face, and yelled, "Good job, Swiper! You brought it back!"

Ugh.

On Being Entitled

While attending a meeting at work, my department secretary came in and said Bradley was on the phone and it was an emergency. I dropped everything and ran out to the office phone, only to have Bradley say, "Can you please stop putting butterscotch chips in my trail mix? They are gross."

Learning Grammar

The boys were lying in the dark, arguing over whether the word *shit* was a noun or a verb.

I know as a good parent I should have gone in there and told them to knock it off, but I was seriously loving that conversation.

Someone's got an Attitude Problem

We were at a traffic light where police were directing traffic,

Bradley: "Mom, what's going on?"

Me: "It's a funeral procession. See, all of the cars are following the hearse to the cemetery."

Bradley: "Who died?"

Me: "How am I supposed to know? I have no idea."

Bradley: "Well, you always say that we can't get away with stuff because you know everything. See, that's just proof that you don't know everything."

Brother Torture

Nate: "Mom, I did a bad thing today."

Me: "What did you do?"

Nate: "I called Bradley a bad name."

Me: "What did you call him?"

Nate: "I called him a baby."

Me: "Why did you call him a baby?"

Nate (bright-eyed and smiling): "I called him a baby because I wanted to experience the pure joy of him getting mad."

On Playing Dumb

When Bradley was four-years-old, I took him to the doctor to get his vaccinations and a checkup before kindergarten was set to start. As part of the report that would be sent to the school, the doctor also had to ask Bradley questions to check that he was intellectually developing as well. She started asking him, "What is your first name? Last name? Middle name? Parents' names?" etc. To my wonderment, for each of the questions, Bradley would shrug his shoulders and simply say, "I don't know."

I sat there with my mouth agape, shocked at what he was saying. The doctor wrote notes on the form, while I sat there in a total panic. When the doctor excused herself from the room for a few moments, I looked at Bradley flabbergasted and said, "Why are you telling her you don't know those things? You know the answers to all of those questions." He looked at me with a sly smile and said, "I am playing a trick on her."

At Least He Thinks Ahead

Nate (11) came home with a note from school, telling parents about a sketchy man in a green SUV who was trying to pick up kids and give them drugs (yikes!).

I read the note, then looked at Nate and said, "So what would you do if this guy drove up next to you and asked you to get in the car, or if you wanted drugs?"

Nate: "I would run away!"

Me: "Good! What would you do if he got a hold of you?"

Nate (pulling some round-edged, little kid scissors out of his pocket): "I brought these home from school and hid them in my pocket, just in case I had to *shank* him."

I Hate it When He is Right

I ordered a boxed set of books for Bradley, and he was desperately checking the mail each day to see if they had arrived. Finally, I got an email from Amazon that said they shipped.

Bradley: "Mom, do you think my books will be here today?"

Me: "No, Bradley. They literally just sent them out last night."

Bradley: "So, there is no chance?"

Me: "Correct. No chance."

Bradley: "Mom, there is always a chance. You can't say with 100% certainty that they won't be here today. I am choosing to hope, even if it's a one in a million shot, there is always hope."

Me: "Well, you can hope all you want, but they said they wouldn't be here for two more days. Face facts. They aren't coming today."

And what shows up on the doorstep that same day? The books.

On Being a Rule-Breaker

On the last day of second grade, Nate cleaned out his desk and brought home all his workbooks and school supplies. The next morning, I heard him giggling away in his bedroom, so I went in to see what all of the fun was about. He had his math workbook out, and with a mischievous smile and giggle, he said, "Mom! I am answering all of the questions wrong on purpose!"

On Using School Resources

Bradley (10): "Mom, we got new dictionaries at school today, and I spent my free time looking up all of the bad words I could find."

Me: "Great. Dare I ask what words you found?"

Bradley: "Well, I found 'jackass' and 'ass', but then I got my dictionary taken away when my friends started doing it too."

Me: "I'm sure your teacher loved that you kids were doing that. What did she say?"

Bradley: "Well, she said that we were being inappropriate, so we snuck the dictionaries out at recess and did it there."

The Bedtime Negotiation

After the boys were acting up at bedtime,

Me: "Your normal bedtime is 8 pm, but we have been letting you stay up late since it is summer. So once it hits 8 pm, you guys are on *our time*. If you start arguing or bugging each other after 8 pm, then you have to go to bed."

Bradley: "So, if after 8 pm is *your time* then everything from waking up until 8 pm is *our time*, and we should be able to do whatever we want."

Future Chief Negotiator

The boys were fighting and pestering each other:

Me: "I am instituting a *no touching policy*! Keep your hands to yourself!"

Bradley: "Mom, maybe we should have a *keep your words to yourself* policy, too."

Me: "Good idea, Bradley. Then maybe you two won't say mean things to each other."

Bradley: "Well, Mom, the no words policy means you, too. Then you'll have to stop bossing us around all of the time."

On Dealing a Low Blow

The boys were fighting over laser guns we got at a garage sale. They both were sent to their room, where they were crying and yelling (through the adjoining wall to each other): "*Baby, baby, you are a baby!*" Which made each of them cry even more hysterically.

Solution: put in the earplugs and call it a day.

On Being Bored

For entertainment one evening, Nate (three) was holding a big, uninflated balloon in his teeth, pulling it out about two feet in front of his face and letting go, snapping himself in the lips. Each time, he would scream "Ouch!" yet he continued to do it over and over again.

Swear Words Galore

When the boys were about seven and nine years old, we were driving in the car, and out of the blue, Nate started hysterically crying. I looked in my rear-view mirror, and asked, "What is wrong, sweetie?" Bradley piped in with, "He is crying because he said a bad word." I asked, "When did you say a bad word, at school?" "No,

I said a bad word just now, in my head." He had gotten so scared to say a bad word, that it was giving him anxiety.

I then proceeded to pull the car over, and said, "Alright, we are in the car with all of the windows rolled up and nobody can hear us. I am giving you each permission, in this safe space, to say any and all of the bad words that you can think of; get them all out while we are here. I don't want you saying these words in front of other people, but if accidentally saying a swear word is making you sad and scared, then we need to get these words out of our system."

The boys just looked at me like I was crazy, and at first, they refused to participate—they thought they would get in trouble for saying the words. I reassured them that they wouldn't get in trouble, and Nate looked at me, and whispered under his breath, "Shiiiiiiiiiiiiiiiit." I said, "Alright, let's really hear it. Say it like you mean it." He then confidently said, "Shit!"

As you can imagine, once the floodgates were open, all three of us were yelling all the bad words the boys knew. They laughed, I laughed, and after that, my boys didn't worry about saying swear words anymore. They never said them at inappropriate times, and quickly learned that there was a time and a place for everything.

Life with Brothers

Me: "Nate, where's Bradley?"

Nate: "In his room hating me."

Dead Fish Named Frank and Beans

Nate: "*Mom*! Frank died yesterday, and now Beans died, too!"

Me: "What? How weird—what do you think happened to them?"

Bradley, shaking his head with a sad look on his face: "I think I figured it out. The only thing it could be: mutual combat."

On Foreseeing the Future

At the beginning of summer, the boys had already run out of things to argue about. So, they began the cute new habit of arguing about *what if* situations. Case in point:

Nate: "*Mom*, Bradley said that if he had $1,000, he wouldn't share it with me!"

Bradley: "Well, it would be *mine*, not his!"

Nate: "*No fair!*"

On Bullying

Nate (four): "Mom, is it going to rain again today?"

Me: "Yes."

Nate: "The rain is mean to me. It gets my shoes wet, and then it hits me in the head."

Uh-Oh

When Bradley was two-years-old, Dave was working in the garage and dropped something on his foot. Without thinking, he yelled "fuck!" at the top of his lungs. After talking to Dave about being careful with his language around Bradley, I spent the next few days nervously waiting to see if Bradley would repeat the word.

After a few weeks, I let out a big sigh of relief, thinking we were in the clear. No such luck. Not that long afterward, Bradley came up to me and said, "Mom, I pooped in my diaper. FUUUCCCKKK!"

He yelled the f-word in the same tone of voice as Dave had yelled it. I turned around so Bradley wouldn't see me laughing and went into the bedroom to immediately call Dave and tell him what happened.

Dave suggested I ignore it until we could figure out what to do. Bradley spent the entire day using the f-word: "I dropped my sippy cup. FUUUCCCKKK!" "Sadie ate my cracker. FUUUCCCKKK!" I mean, seriously, it lasted *all day long*. And I never reacted—not even in the slightest. We woke up the next morning, expecting to be forced to deal with this nightmare head-on, but luckily, the urge had passed and he didn't say it again (at least until he was a teenager).

A Good Lie

As ambulance sirens sound in the distance,

Bradley: "What is that sound?"

Me: "It is the sirens of a police car coming to get you and Nate."

Bradley: "Why would they come to get us?"

Me: "Because you two won't stop fighting, so I called them to come and arrest you for disturbing the peace."

As the sirens are getting closer and louder,

Bradley: "Call them and tell them to stop! We will stop fighting!"

Me: "I don't believe you. You two always say that you will stop fighting, and you never do."

Bradley (grabbing Nate and hugging him): "We will stop! We will stop!"

#MeanMom

Boy Games

My boys enjoy playing the let's-spray-each-other-in-the-wiener-with-the-power-hose-to-see-who-cries-first game. They love anything involving pain and seeing who cries first. Different variations of the game have included holding a rubber band on their chin, pulling the other end out about two feet, and snapping their face to see who cries first. A third variation they love is playing Don't Break the Ice and using the ice hammer to whack each other in the testicles to see who cries first. The list goes on and on...

Brotherly Love

Bradley: "Mom, Nate won't play with me. I am sorry to tell you that you wasted a whole lotta labor pains having him since now you still have to play with me since Nate won't."

All Good Things Must Come to an End

When the boys were two and four-years-old, I ordered a ladybug growing kit from an educational catalog; you know, where they send you everything that you need to watch the ladybugs develop, starting with the habitat and the eggs. Every day for about a month, we watched with anticipation as the ladybugs moved through their lifecycle, and we became very attached to the eggs, larvae, pupa, and finally, mature ladybugs! We were so excited once the five or so ladybugs hatched that we decided to throw a ladybug party so all the kids in the neighborhood who had come over daily to check on the ladybugs' development could celebrate with us.

I baked a ladybug shaped cake, everyone wore black, red, and white clothes, and we had ladybug shaped food. We decided the culminating moment of the party would be when we opened the little ladybug habitat and let all the mature ladybugs free! The time finally came, and parents and kids all gathered around, excitedly waiting for the ladybug release.

I opened the top of the habitat, thinking that they would all fly out. Nope; it can never be that easy. So, I reached my hand in and gently picked up each ladybug and put them in the palm of my hand, expecting to walk over to a tree or bush and set them on a leaf. I knelt down one last time so all of the kids could see the ladybugs up close, and out comes Nate's little fat finger, and *squishes* all of the ladybugs; dead in one fell swoop. The kids all started crying, and of course, all the parents were trying hard not to burst into fits of laughter. The party was a (funny, not funny) bust.

On Seeing The Hunger Games DVD at the Grocery Store

Nate: "Mom, is *The Hunger Games* a story about someone who is really hungry, so they participate in an eating contest?"

Me: "No, it is a story about people who have very little and are starving, and each city has to compete against each other, and they kill each other. It is inappropriate for kids. That's why we haven't read the book."

Nate (after thinking about it for a while): "So, they like, shoot each other for Skittles?"

Me: "You know; something like that."

On Helping the Environment

I was helping Bradley (five) with his homework, and one of the questions he had to answer was, "How do you conserve electricity?" His answer: "When we ignore the phone calls from the telemarketers and don't answer the phone."

On Spotting a Druggie

Driving in the car with the boys,

Bradley: "Mom, look at that car in front of us. That guy is smoking weed."

Me: "What are you talking about? How can you tell that he is smoking weed? You don't know what weed smoking looks like."

Bradley: "I know what weed smoking looks like. I've been to Walmart enough to know."

When They Act Too Old for Their Own Good

Nate (three) was climbing up on a tall bar stool to wash his hands at the kitchen sink. He was at that stage where he said, "I do it!" to everything and never wanted any help. As we were all watching the impending danger, Bradley grinned and said, "Well this oughta be good."

I'm Smarter than You

We were driving with the family, and Bradley and I were having a disagreement.

Dave (frustrated): "Funny, Bradley, you are only eight-years-old and already think you know more than your mom."

Bradley (pausing for a moment to think): "Dad, I actually know more than you, too."

On Understanding Drugs

Nate came home from kindergarten with a bookmark that he made that said, "Apples are better than drugs."

Me: "That is so true, Nate. Apples *are* better than drugs."

Nate: "Mom, what are drugs?" (Mind you, the school did a huge campaign on how drugs are dangerous, but he had no idea what drugs were).

Me: "Well, drugs are things like pills or like a needle filled with yucky liquid that people put in their body to make them feel good. But, although they make you feel good, they are bad for your body, make you sick, make you lose all your money, cause problems in your family, can make your hair fall out, and can make your teeth all fall out, too, so they are bad."

Nate: (looking wide-eyed): "Well, if your teeth all fall out then you would make tons of money from the tooth fairy. That would be cool."

On the Premise of Fifty Shades of Grey

When I was reading the *Fifty Shades of Grey* Trilogy,

Bradley: "What is your book about?"

Me: "It is about a man and a woman, both who have never been in love, trying to figure out how to make their relationship work."

Bradley: "Why is it called *Fifty Shades of Grey*?"

Me: "Well, the male character seems to have lots of different personalities, and she can never figure him out, so she calls him *Fifty Shades*."

Now, whenever I (or a friend of his) says to Bradley something similar to, "Stop acting so crazy," he replies with "Yep. I'm *Fifty Shades*."

I have been getting a lot of sideways glances from mothers.

On Having Money

Nate: "Mom, how many bucks is a *fortune?*"

Me: "How many bucks do you think a fortune is?"

Nate: "Ten bucks."

Me: "Yep, you're right! We must be rich!"

On Living in a Nice Neighborhood

Nate (while we were driving, looking up at the fancy houses on the hill): "Mommy, that is big house land up there. We live down in small house land."

Me (chuckling): "Do you wish we lived in *big house land?*"

Nate: "No. I think *small house land* is way more fun."

On Knowing How to Use Tools

Bradley, a fisherman's son, when asked by his Cub Scout leader what needle-nosed pliers are for, answered: "to pull a fish hook out of someone's hand."

On Where to Spread Your Ashes After You Die

Bradley (six): "Mom, what does *cremation* mean?"

Me (after explaining what it was) added: "Your ashes usually get spread somewhere that is special to you that holds important meaning to you in your heart, like the ocean, the mountains, or your favorite fishing hole."

Me (after discussing where Dave and I want our ashes spread): "Bradley, where would you want your ashes spread?"

Bradley: "In Walmart."

Parents are Overrated

Bradley (five): "I already know everything. I don't need parents."

Party Poopers

Me: "Boys! We are going to have a cleaning party! We are going to crank the music, dance, and have snacks while we clean! *Whoohoo!*"

Bradley, with a sad look on his face: "Mom, I don't want to hurt your feelings, but you're going to be all alone because nobody is going to come to your party."

On Being Bilingual

The boys and I were discussing graffiti this morning over breakfast.

Bradley: "I saw some graffiti on the back of the bathroom door when we were camping, but I don't understand why they always write graffiti in Chinese so I can't read it."

On Committing a Felony

Bradley: "Mom, when you kill plants, does that count as murder?"

Me: "No, Bradley."

Bradley: "Good, because if it was murder, you would go to jail for a long time."

Kids and Messy Rooms

Me: "Bradley, we need to clean up this bedroom. It is a total disaster."

Bradley (five): "*Mom! I am* going to clean it up. I'm just going to wait until I'm a teenager."

Infamous for Murder

Bradley came home from school asking me about murder,

Bradley: "You know, not everyone who gets convicted of murder goes to prison. Some become singers instead."

Me: "What are you talking about?"

Bradley: "You know, Mom, like that guy who sings the song, 'I shot a man in Reno, just to watch him die.' Now he's a famous singer."

On Getting What You Want

The boys and I were making a cake, and as I was making the frosting:

Bradley (whispering and swinging a necklace from side to side): "You will obey."

Bradley (after a moment): "Can we eat more chocolate frosting?"

Me: "No."

Bradley (in a disgusted voice under his breath): "Dangit; I guess my hypnosis didn't work."

The Heart Rules

The boys were fighting over who got to ride which scooter,

Me: "Bradley, why don't you just be the cool big brother and let Nate have the scooter that he wants."

Bradley: "Mom, it is up to my heart whether I let him have it or not, and my heart is in charge of my brain who makes that decision. I'm sorry, but my heart says no."

Tell That Girl Who is Boss

Bradley: "Mom, someone at school said something mean to me. A girl said, 'Girls go to college to get more knowledge, and boys go to Jupiter to get more stupider.'"

Me: "Well you tell them that they are the stupid one for saying *more stupider* because that's not how you say it, you just say *stupid* instead of *more stupider*."

He just looked at me, shook his head, and said, "Mom, can you just stop talking now?"

Reflections from Mom

Man, boys have such an active imagination! Testing limits are something that I respect in a child. It is a bit annoying when they are young, but if you think about it, these are the skills that we want to cultivate in our children for them to be successful adults. We want our kids to be able to stand up for themselves, have a voice, and to be able to negotiate their differences with others. When they negotiate differences with us, it is not so fun, I know. But when I get frustrated, I like to think of the big-picture life skills they are practicing. This is the only way I can keep my sanity.

Epilogue

I found such great happiness in not only cat-aloging the exchanges you just read, but also from reading them again with my boys now that they are older. As Bradley and Nate entered the teen years, I continued to keep track of our funny exchanges and decided to include some excerpts here, for you to enjoy. Because their teen years are just beginning, I know I have a lot of work ahead keeping track of their stories; however, I couldn't help sharing some of the early stages of awkwardness and hilarity of them being teens with you. So here is a sneak peek at the teen version of our conversations.

Appendix A

The Teen Years

When Mom Leaves Out a Key Detail About Sex Education

I was at home grading papers on my computer, and I decided to take a break and check my social media. While I was scrolling, a post from a parent group at Bradley's school popped up, and I saw that many parents were losing their minds over the upcoming seventh grade sex education curriculum due to start the next day.

Nobody was specific about what they were upset about, but man, were they on fire. I decided to investigate further, and sent a private message to one of my friends who was in the discussion to see what she knew. She said, "You might want to check the curriculum. It's pretty major." "What's the big deal?" I asked, "It can't be that bad." Her response: "They will be learning how to put condoms on a wooden model of a penis." "Um, okay, that does seem like it might be a big deal—I remember learning how to put condoms on a banana in sex ed, so I get that people might be uncomfortable with that." "That is not even the worst part; it is *co-ed*."

Ah…now I understood. I thought about this a little bit and decided to give Bradley a heads-up so he wouldn't be surprised, and let him decide if he wanted to attend. When the permission slips about the week-long sex-ed program had come home the week before, there was an opt-out choice. I told Bradley that I would be shocked if they talked about anything that he didn't already know, but if for any reason he felt uncomfortable, we could opt him out.

Bradley came home from school a few hours later, and I called him into the kitchen for a talk. "You know your sex-ed curriculum starts tomorrow?" "Yes." "Well, there are a bunch of parents who are upset about the lessons and are not allowing their kids to attend." "Really? What's the big deal?" "Well, you will be learning how to put condoms on." "Okay, that's weird." "I know."

"But the part that parents are more upset about is that it is co-ed, so the girls will be there, learning how to put condoms on, too, so it might be kind of awkward." "*Why* in the *world* would girls need to learn how to put condoms on? They don't even have a *penis*." "I know, I know, but think about it, Bradley. These girls may grow up and want to be intimate with a man, and maybe the man won't know how to put a condom on, so they need to learn how to put the condom on too, so they can protect themselves if necessary." "That is totally creepy and gross." "I understand, but it is what it is, the girls need to practice putting condoms on, too, so you all will be doing it together. Just try to get over the weirdness, if you can." Bradley crinkled up his nose, and with a worried look on his face, left to go work on his homework.

Over the next hour, I noticed that Bradley was walking around acting weird, wringing his hands and looking at the floor. Later, while I was in the bathroom washing my face, he came in saying that he needed to talk to me. "Mom,

I think I need to opt-out of sex-ed." "Really? Okay, that is fine. But why?" After taking a deep breath, "Mom. I *cannot* have the girls practicing putting condoms on me in front of everyone in the classroom!"

On Barely Being Able to Take It

Me: "Bradley, what did you learn during your first day of sex-ed?"

Brad: "I learned that I wanted to die."

On Escaping

Me: "What's on the Sunday agenda, boys?"

Bradley: "Relaxing and enjoying a day without sex-ed."

On Reading into Things Too Much

Nate and I were watching The Voice, and a Pantene commercial came on where the lady was flinging her hair around.

Nate: "It is clear that she is about to have sex."

On Having to Explain License Plate Frames

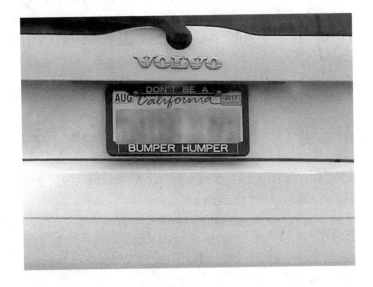

I was driving Bradley (13) to school, and we saw this license plate frame in front of us: "Don't be a bumper humper."

Bradley: "Mom, what does that mean? What is a *bumper humper?*"

Me: "You took sex-ed. What do you think it means?"

Bradley: "I'm not sure, but I think that it means the person driving the car is telling you not to have crazy sex with people that you don't know."

Me: "Good guess, but no. Think about how close people have to be when they are having sex. They have to be right up on each other for it to work, right? Now, what do you think it means?"

Bradley: "I don't know. Just tell me please."

Me: "It means that this person doesn't want you driving so close to their bumper that it is like humping them. They don't want your car right on top of their car."

Bradley: "Well that is disgusting. Why does everything have to be about sex? Cars can't even have sex."

A few minutes later we were driving down a different street, and we came up to a stoplight and I pulled up closely to the car in front of us.

Bradley, laughing hysterically: "Mom, quit humping that guy's bumper!"

Everything is About Sex

Every morning I make Bradley a banana with peanut butter to go with his breakfast. I had noticed that lately, he closed his eyes while he ate it. I assumed he was just enjoying it, but I finally asked him why he closed his eyes.

Bradley: "After sex-ed, I just can't even look at a banana the same way ever again."

On Lady Issues

Nate: "Mom, what is feminine odor? They keep talking about it in that commercial."

Me: "Well, you know how sometimes your junk stinks?"

Nate: "Yeah."

Me: "Well, sometimes a lady's private parts stink, too, so that is a cleaner to help with that problem."

Bradley: "My life is officially over; I can't un-hear that."

Now That Would Be Interesting

Bradley: "Mom, what are the *Vagina Monologues*? Is that where the doctor sticks a Q-tip up a woman's vagina to see if anything is wrong?"

On Proper Masculine Hygiene

Bradley: "If I have a hairy chest when I get older, is there anything I can do about it?"

Dave: "You can get a Brazilian wax job."

Me: "Um, no; a Brazilian is not for chest hair."

Nate: "Well, what's it for?"

Me: "It's for pubic hair."

Loooooong pause...

Nate: "Wait, what?" People yank out their pubic hair with wax?"

Me: "Yes. Some people do."

Nate: "It's official—I never want to grow up. Ever."

Bradley: "Everything that was holy inside me is dead."

I Told You So

I took the boys out to dinner, and when the server brought our drinks to the table, he said to Bradley and Nate, "You boys are old enough to have adult drink glasses, correct?"

Me, jokingly, "I'm not so sure about that. The older one is in puberty, and he is clumsy."

The guy just started cracking up, passed out our drinks, and as soon as Bradley tilted his glass back to take the first sip, he spilled half of his soda all over his shirt.

Proceed with Caution

Bradley was in the boys' shared bedroom being a grumpy, emotional teenager:

Nate (10): "Mom, can I go into our bedroom? I need to get something."

Me: "Sure, but be careful."

Nate quietly entered their room, got his head bitten off, then walked out of the room mumbling under his breath "Damn puberty."

Moody, Irritable, and Not so Nice

Nate: "Bradley's all crabby and full of hemorrhoids."

Me: "What the heck are you talking about?"

Nate: "You know, that teenager stuff."

Me: "Ooh, you mean *hormones*."

Teenage Music Taste

Nate: "Mom, can you download that Justin Bieber song from The Karate Kid?

Me: "Sure."

Bradley: "*No*! I hate Justin Bieber! The only people who listen to Justin Bieber are six-year-old girls and 40-year-olds who still live with their moms."

A Sure-Proof Way to Get a Pack of Teenage Boys to Be Quiet

I was driving Bradley and a pack of his friends around, and they were all arguing and yelling and wouldn't be quiet.

Me: I know, boys! Let's play the game *Did You Know?* I'll start! Did you know I started my period when I was 12?"

You could cut the awkward silence with a knife.

On Learning About the Birds and the Bees

When Rowdy was a puppy, she was very attached to her stuffed killer whale. One day, after air humping it for five minutes, Bradley said, "I think Rowdy just got to second base with that orca."

The Perpetually Grumpy Teenager

Bradley: "What is the Halloween Witch going to give me this year in exchange for all of my Halloween candy?"

Me: "She just picked something off of your birthday wish list, Bradley."

Bradley: "She probably picked the cheapest thing on the list, and I am giving her all of my candy!"

Me: "Why don't you wait to see what she gives you before you complain about it? Jeez."

Bradley: "I'm just complaining about the fact that I have to complain."

On Being Entitled

Bradley was acting like an entitled a-hole, so Dave asked him to look up the word *entitlement* and explain to us what he thought it meant. This is what he wrote: Entitlement means *the fact of having the right to do something*. If you don't believe me, Google it. It means to me, that I have the right to do whatever I want."

On Avoiding Exercise at All Costs

Me: "How come you never go to any of the school dances?"

Bradley: "I hate those dances."

Me: "Why?"

Bradley: "Because all that we do is jump around in the hot gym and get sweaty. It is basically PE."

He Has No Idea

Bradley (13): "Mom, why can't I watch rated R movies?"

Me: "You're too young to see all of that nudity and stuff."

Him: "Well, I took showers with you when I was little, so I have already seen it all."

It's Kind of True

Bradley at Costco: "This is an alcoholic's dream."

On Making Innocent Situations Inappropriate

We were decorating Christmas cookies, and Bradley accidentally spilled red sprinkles on the crotch of his gingerbread cookie. He immediately started calling it the "period cookie" and was beside himself in hysterics.

Acknowledgements

Thank you so much for reading my book! This project was a labor of love, and as I mentioned before, it took almost 10 years to write. I always knew I wanted to share my experiences with my boys with others, and thanks to a handful of amazing people, I have finally been able to do just that.

I must start first by thanking Dave, Bradley, and Nate because, without them, I wouldn't have any material! The three of them are my heart and soul, and I couldn't have done this without their ongoing support. I also want to thank my family and friends who continually supported and encouraged me to write down my stories and share them with the world. Without their encouragement, I would have been too scared to take the leap to get my book published. And lastly, I would like to thank Kary Oberbrunner, my Author Academy Elite coach, who helped me tell my story and answered all of my pains-taking questions about writing with patience and grace.

So many times in life, we get consumed by negativity. My goal was to put some joy out into the world. I hope I was successful.

Endnotes

1 Donna Matthews, Ph.D., "Call Children's Private Body Parts What They Are," *Psychology Today,* March 6, 2017, https://www.psychologytoday.com/blog/going-beyond-intelligence/201703/call-children-s-private-body-parts-what-they-are

2 Laura Palumbo, "Creating Campaigns for Change," *The National Sexual Violence Resource Center,* December 6, 2015, https://www.nsvrc.org/blogs/saam/healthy-sexuality

3 Deborah Tannen, Ph. D., *You Just Don't Understand: Women and Men in Conversation* (William Morrow Paperbacks, 2007).

4   Daniel Goleman, Ph.D., *Emotional Intelligence: Why it Can Matter More Than IQ* (Bantam Books, 2005).

5   Tracy Gleason, Ph.D., "Why Make-Believe is an Important Part of Childhood Development," *The Conversation*, April 6, 20

About the Author

Diane Auten learned the importance of communicating effectively when she earned first her bachelor's and then a master's degree in communication studies. Today, Diane is a full-time college professor, professional speaker, and consultant in the area  of communication. Her areas of expertise are in business and professional communication as well as interpersonal relationships. Her favorite presentation topics include family communication, public speaking, email communication, social media, networking, first impressions, gender communication, and body language. Inspiring, fun, and always engaging, Diane brings a wealth of fresh, interactive techniques to every audience.

Diane is also a mother with ample opportunities to test her communication skills! As you have read, she has two sons, Bradley and Nate, as well as her life-of-the-party-husband Dave. She lives on the beautiful Central Coast of California where she also enjoys cooking, camping, teaching Zumba, and spending time with her dogs.

Connect at: DianeAuten.com